ORIGAMI TREASURE CHEST

CONTENTS

Published by Graph-sha Ltd., Tokyo, Japan.
Overseas distributor: Japan Publications Trading Co., Ltd., P.O.Box 5030 Tokyo International, Tokyo, Japan.
Distributors:
UNITED STATES: Kodansha America, Inc., through Farrar, Straus & Giroux, 19 Union Square West, New York, NY 10003. BRITISH ISLES AND EUROPEAN CONTINENT: Premier Book Marketing Ltd., 1 Gower Street, London, WC1E 6HA. AUSTRALIA AND NEW ZEALAND: Bookwise International, 54 Crittenden Road, Findon, South Australia 5023.

First edition: March 1991
10 9 8 7 6 5
ISBN: 0-87040-868-2
Printed in Japan

1
ANIMALS

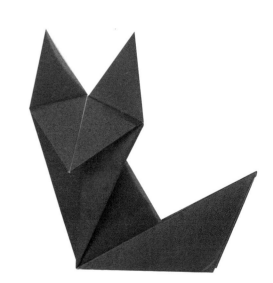

DOG

Fold the head and the body separately and combine them. Easy and simple, and lovely.

BODY

①

⑧

Open and fold.

②

⑦ Inside reverse fold at (b) and pull out the tail.

HEAD

Make a crease in the center to make a nose.

①

④

③ Decide the body size.

⑥ Inside reverse fold at (a).
a
b

②

④ Shape the tail.

③

⑤ Unfold.

◆--- Valley fold　—··— Mountain fold

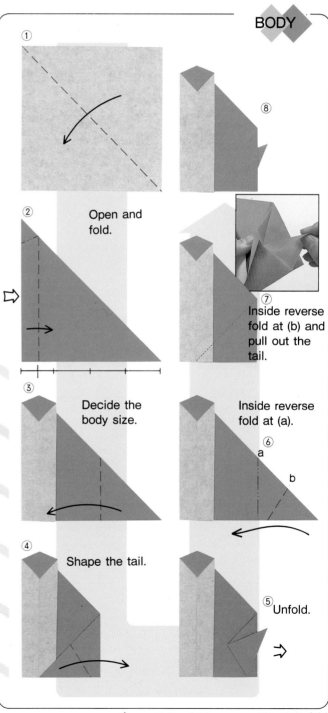

ELEPHANT

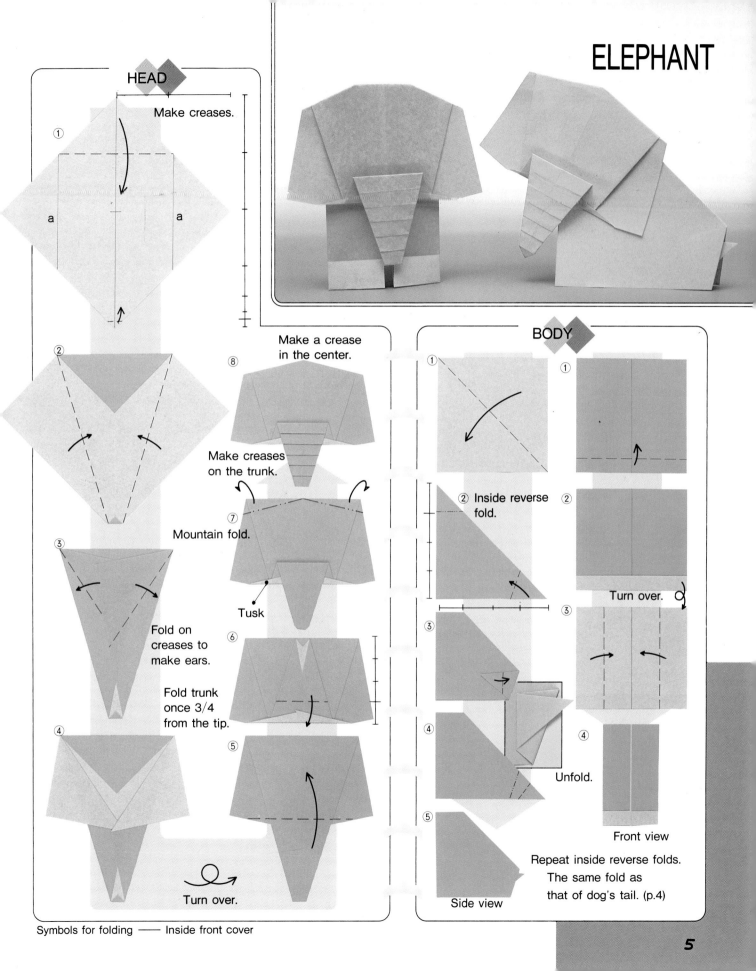

HEAD

① Make creases.

a   a

②

③ Fold on creases to make ears.

④ Turn over.

Make a crease in the center.

⑧ Make creases on the trunk.

⑦ Mountain fold.

Tusk

⑥ Fold trunk once 3/4 from the tip.

⑤

BODY

①

② Inside reverse fold.

③

④ Unfold.

⑤ Side view

Repeat inside reverse folds. The same fold as that of dog's tail. (p.4)

①

② Turn over.

③

④ Front view

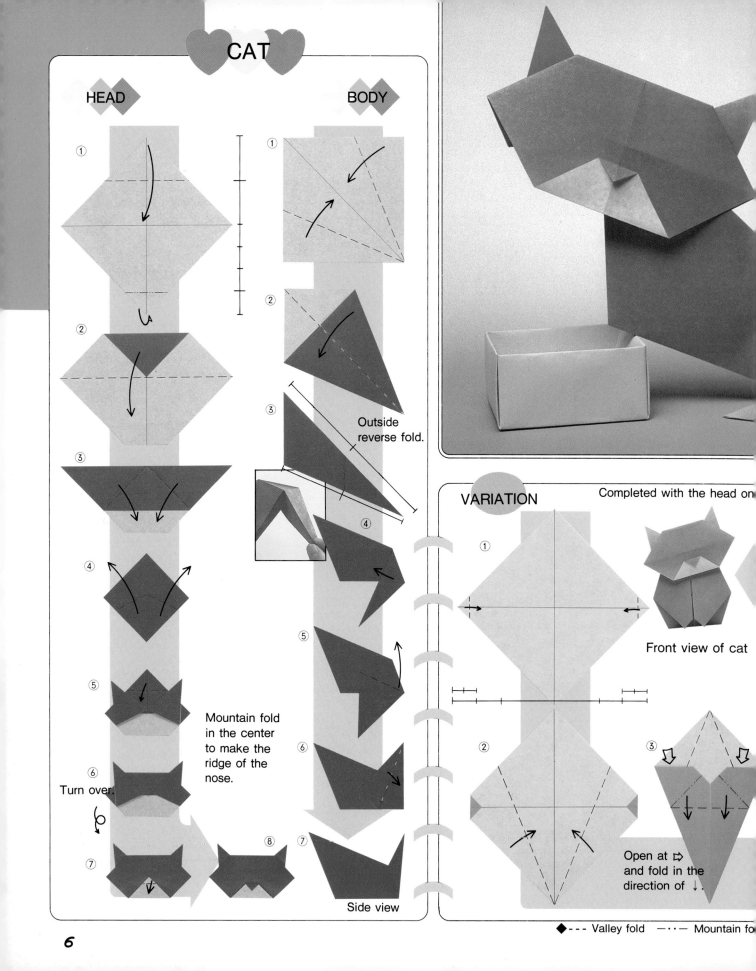

CAT

HEAD

①

②

③

④

⑤

⑥ Turn over.

⑦

Mountain fold in the center to make the ridge of the nose.

BODY

①

② Outside reverse fold.

③

④

⑤

⑥

⑦

⑧ Side view

VARIATION

①

②

③ Open at ⬜▷ and fold in the direction of ↓.

Front view of cat

Completed with the head on

◆--- Valley fold   —·-— Mountain fo

CAT & MOUSE

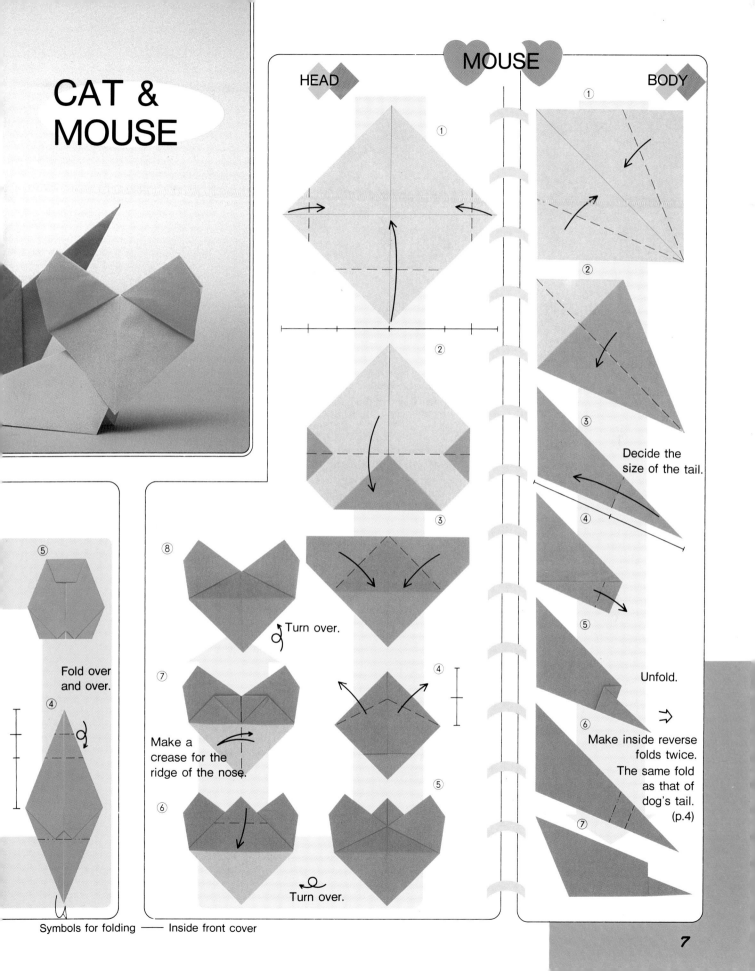

HEAD

① ② ③ ④ ⑤

BODY

① ② ③

Decide the size of the tail.

④ ⑤

Unfold.

⑥ Make inside reverse folds twice. The same fold as that of dog's tail. (p.4)

⑦

⑧ Turn over.

⑦ Make a crease for the ridge of the nose.

④

⑤

⑥ Turn over.

⑤ Fold over and over.

④

Symbols for folding —— Inside front cover

7

HEAD

PANDA

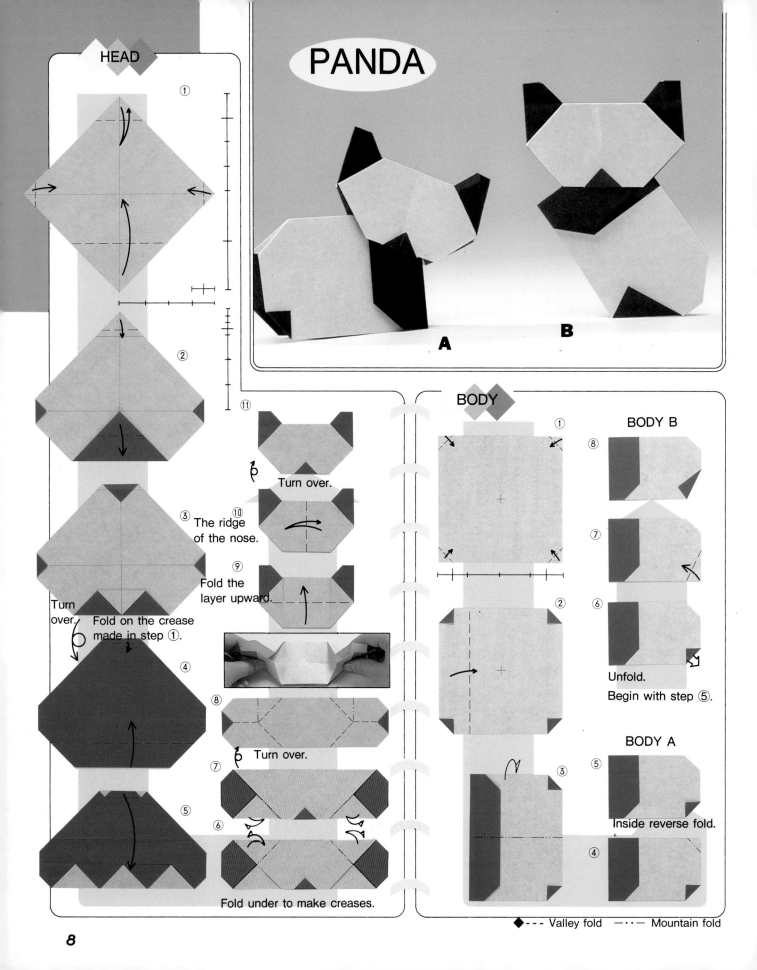

A

B

①

②

③ The ridge of the nose.

Turn over. Fold on the crease made in step ①.

④

⑤

⑪

⑩

⑨ Fold the layer upward.

Turn over.

⑧

⑦

⑥ Fold under to make creases.

BODY

①

②

③

④

⑤ Inside reverse fold.

BODY A

BODY B

⑧

⑦

⑥ Unfold. Begin with step ⑤.

◆--- Valley fold   —·— Mountain fold

8

REINDEER

HEAD

Use a half sheet of paper.

① Make creases.

② Make creases.

Turn over.

③ Fold over and over.

④

Turn over.

⑤

⑥ Fold on the crease made in step ②.

⑦ Pull out to produce the form shown in step ⑧.

⑧

⑨

⑩

⑪ Insert here the tip of the neck.

⑫ Turn over.

The paper before folding

Head	Body

⑬

⑫ Fold inward.

⑪ Make inside reverse folds twice.

(The same as on page 4)

⑩ Unfold.

Open and fold.

⑨ Decide the size of the tail.

⑧

BODY

①

② Turn over.

③

④ Make a crease.

⑤

⑥

⑦

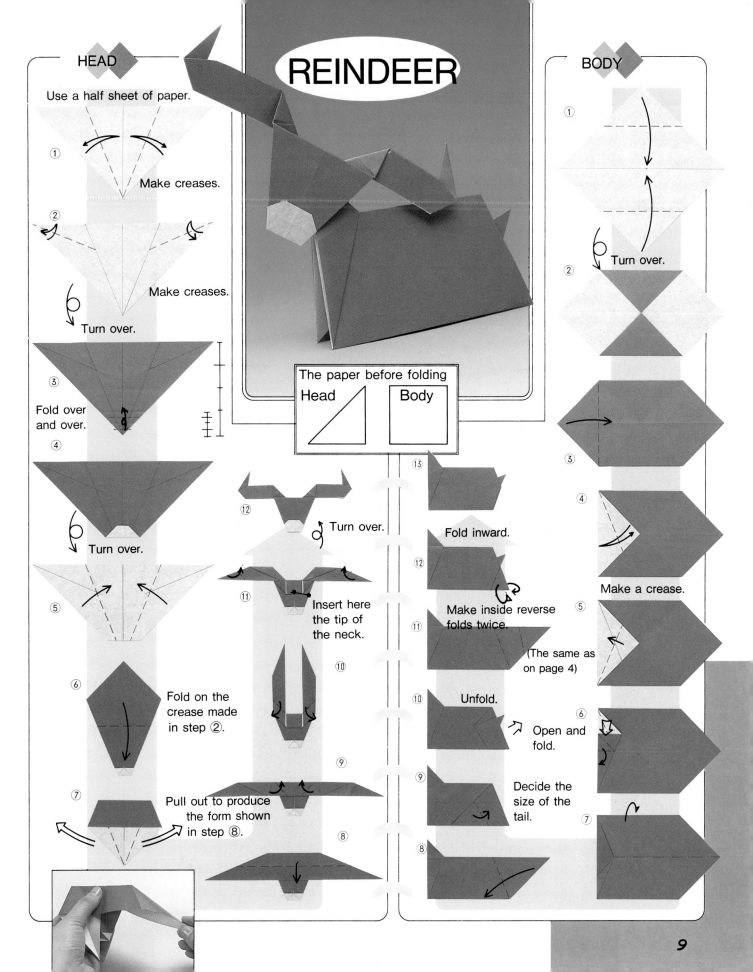

DOGS

B Long-tailed dog

A Short-tailed dog

C Tall dog

DOG (A)

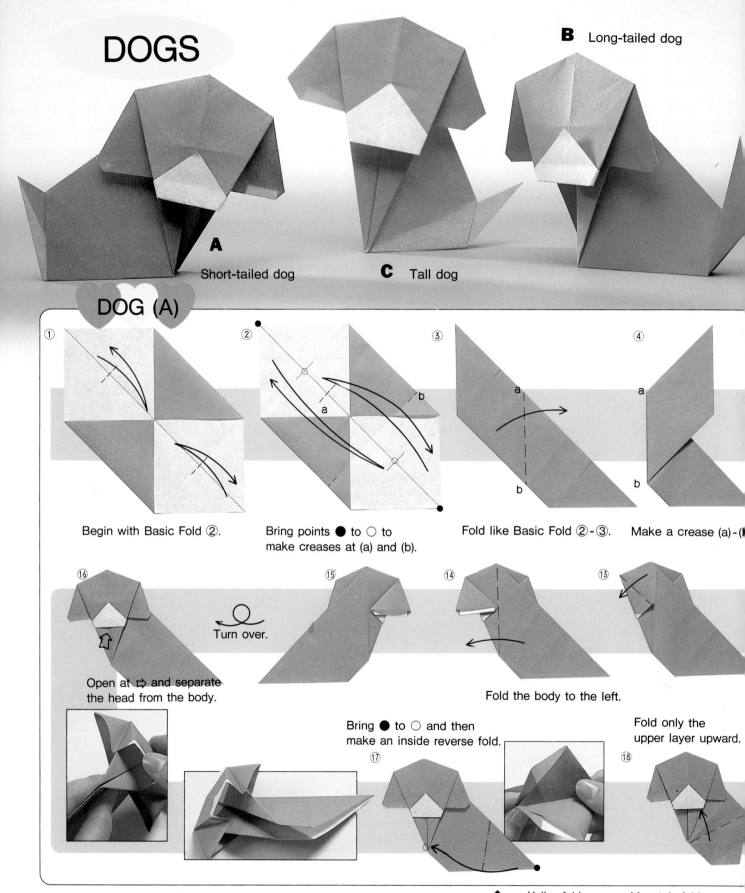

① Begin with Basic Fold ②.

② Bring points ● to ○ to make creases at (a) and (b).

③ Fold like Basic Fold ②-③.

④ Make a crease (a)-(

⑯ Open at ⇨ and separate the head from the body.

⑮ Turn over.

⑭ Fold the body to the left.

⑬

Bring ● to ○ and then make an inside reverse fold.

⑰

Fold only the upper layer upward.

⑱

◆--- Valley fold   —·— Mountain fold

Basic folds of dog, bear & cat.

The first steps are almost the same, and you can produce a dog, a bear and a cat with only a little modification.

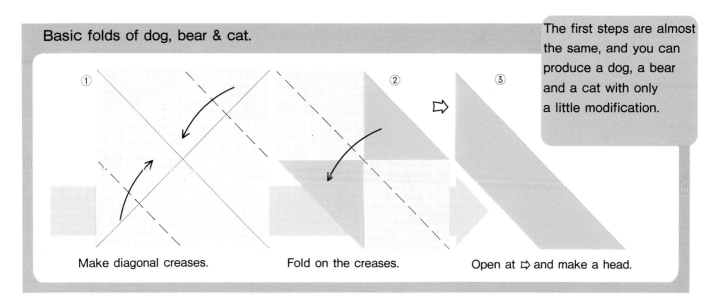

① Make diagonal creases.

② Fold on the creases.

③ Open at ▷ and make a head.

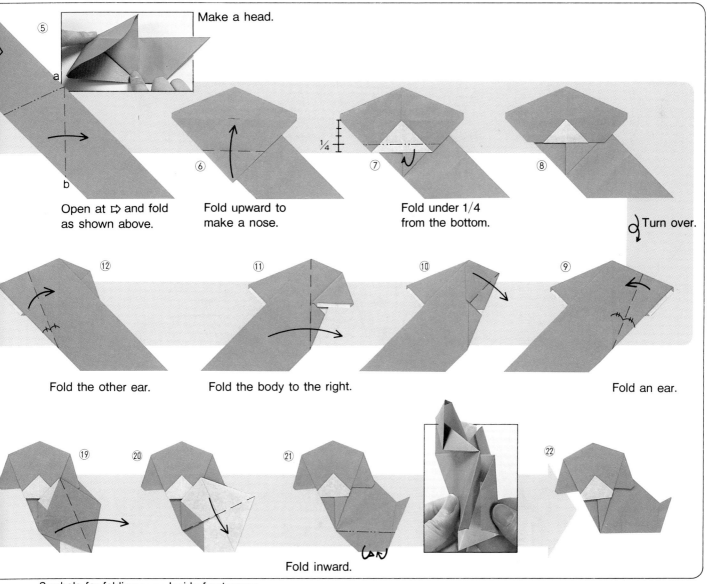

Make a head.

⑤ Open at ▷ and fold as shown above.

⑥ Fold upward to make a nose.

⑦ Fold under 1/4 from the bottom.

⑧

Turn over.

⑫ Fold the other ear.

⑪ Fold the body to the right.

⑩

⑨ Fold an ear.

⑲

⑳

㉑ Fold inward.

㉒

DOG (B)

See page 10 for the completed dog. Begin with step ⑰ of Dog (A) on page 10.

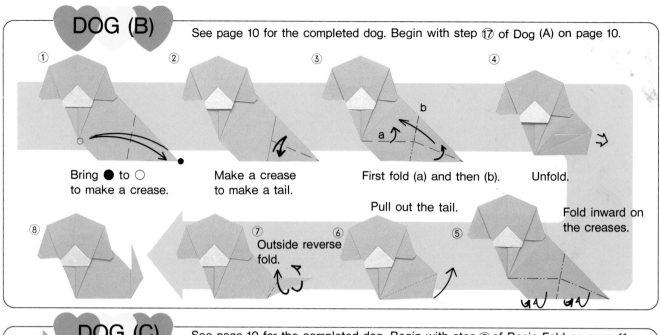

① Bring ● to ○ to make a crease.

② Make a crease to make a tail.

③ First fold (a) and then (b).

④ Unfold.

⑤ Fold inward on the creases.

⑥ Pull out the tail.

⑦ Outside reverse fold.

⑧

DOG (C)

See page 10 for the completed dog. Begin with step ③ of Basic Fold on page 11.

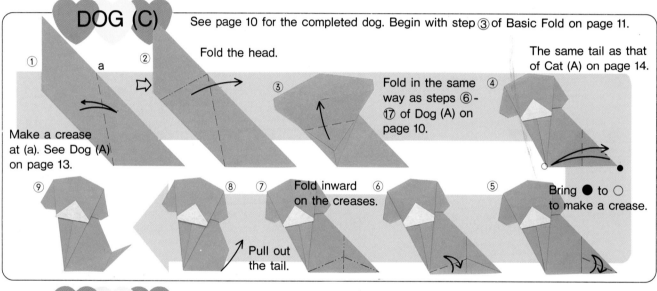

① Make a crease at (a). See Dog (A) on page 13.

② Fold the head.

③ Fold in the same way as steps ⑥ - ⑰ of Dog (A) on page 10.

④ The same tail as that of Cat (A) on page 14.

⑤ Bring ● to ○ to make a crease.

⑥ Fold inward on the creases.

⑦ Pull out the tail.

⑧

⑨

BEAR (B)

See page 13 for the completed bear.

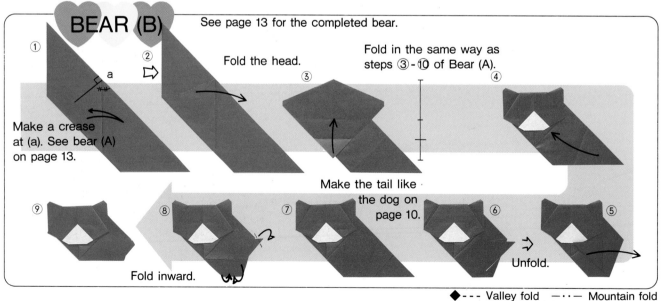

① Make a crease at (a). See bear (A) on page 13.

② Fold the head.

③ Fold in the same way as steps ③ - ⑩ of Bear (A).

④ Make the tail like the dog on page 10.

⑤ Unfold.

⑥

⑦

⑧ Fold inward.

⑨

◆--- Valley fold —·— Mountain fold

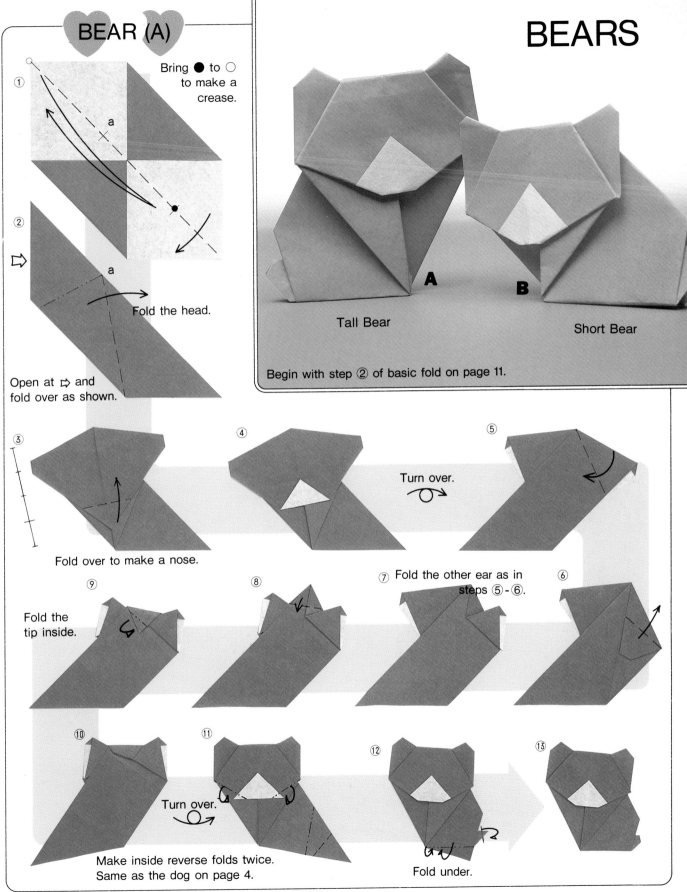

BEAR (A)

BEARS

Tall Bear

Short Bear

① Bring ● to ○ to make a crease.

a

② Open at ⇨ and fold over as shown.

a

Fold the head.

Begin with step ② of basic fold on page 11.

③ Fold over to make a nose.

④

⑤ Turn over.

⑥

⑦ Fold the other ear as in steps ⑤ - ⑥.

⑧

⑨ Fold the tip inside.

⑩

⑪ Turn over.

Make inside reverse folds twice.
Same as the dog on page 4.

⑫ Fold under.

⑬

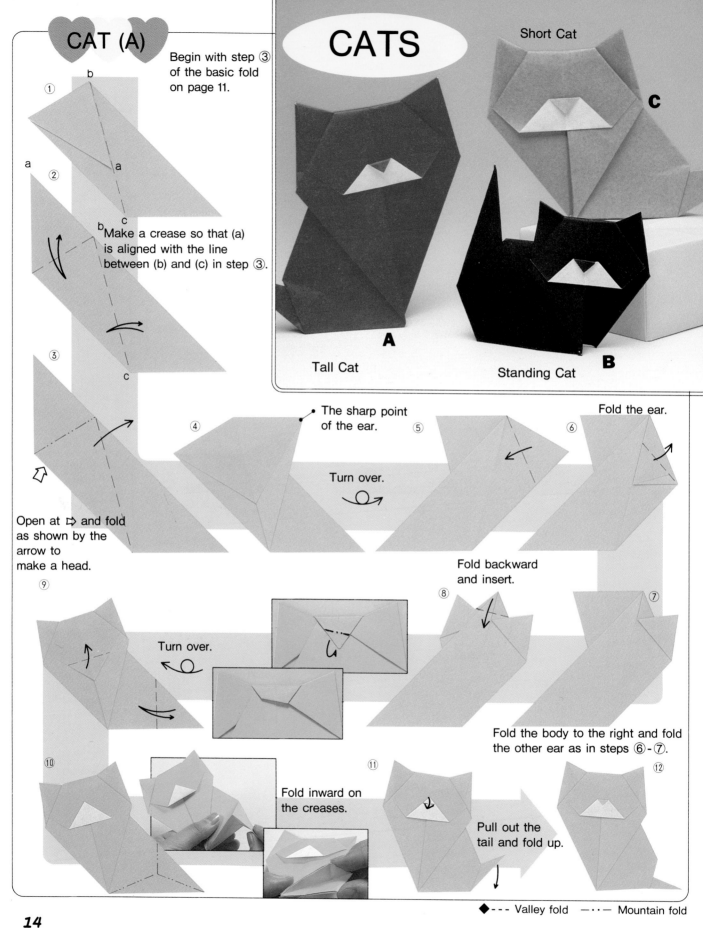

CAT (A)

Begin with step ③ of the basic fold on page 11.

CATS

Short Cat

C

A

Tall Cat

B

Standing Cat

① b

② a | a

b
c

Make a crease so that (a) is aligned with the line between (b) and (c) in step ③.

③ b
c

Open at ⇨ and fold as shown by the arrow to make a head.

④ • The sharp point of the ear.

Turn over.

⑤

⑥ Fold the ear.

Fold backward and insert.

⑦

⑧

Fold the body to the right and fold the other ear as in steps ⑥-⑦.

⑨ Turn over.

⑩ Fold inward on the creases.

⑪ Pull out the tail and fold up.

⑫

◆--- Valley fold   —·— Mountain fold

CAT (B)

The folding method is a little different from (A) and (C).

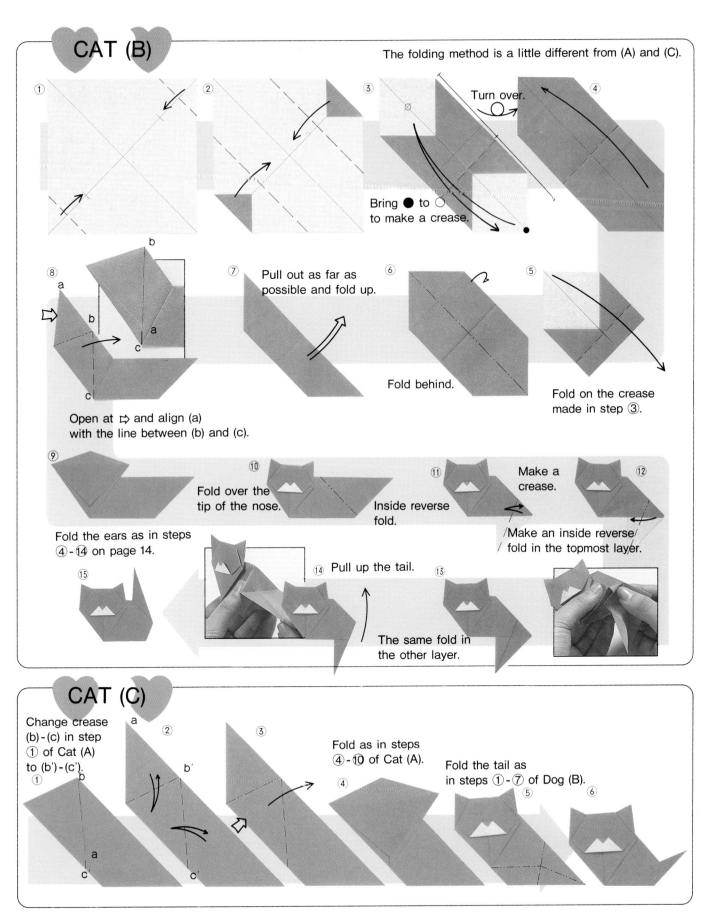

① ② ③ Turn over. ④

Bring ● to ○ to make a crease.

⑧ ⑦ Pull out as far as possible and fold up. ⑥ ⑤

Fold behind.

Fold on the crease made in step ③.

b
a
b
a
c
c

Open at ⇨ and align (a) with the line between (b) and (c).

⑨ ⑩ Fold over the tip of the nose. ⑪ Make a crease. ⑫

Inside reverse fold.

Make an inside reverse fold in the topmost layer.

Fold the ears as in steps ④-⑭ on page 14.

⑮ ⑭ Pull up the tail. ⑬

The same fold in the other layer.

CAT (C)

Change crease (b)-(c) in step ① of Cat (A) to (b')-(c').

① ② ③ Fold as in steps ④-⑩ of Cat (A). ④

Fold the tail as in steps ①-⑦ of Dog (B).

⑤ ⑥

a
b
b'
a
c'
c'

Symbols for folding —— Inside front cover

FOX

KOALA

RABBIT

Koala (See page 19)

Little Fox

Sister Fox

Rabbit (See page 18)

The Basic folds of the Fox, Rabbit and Koala.

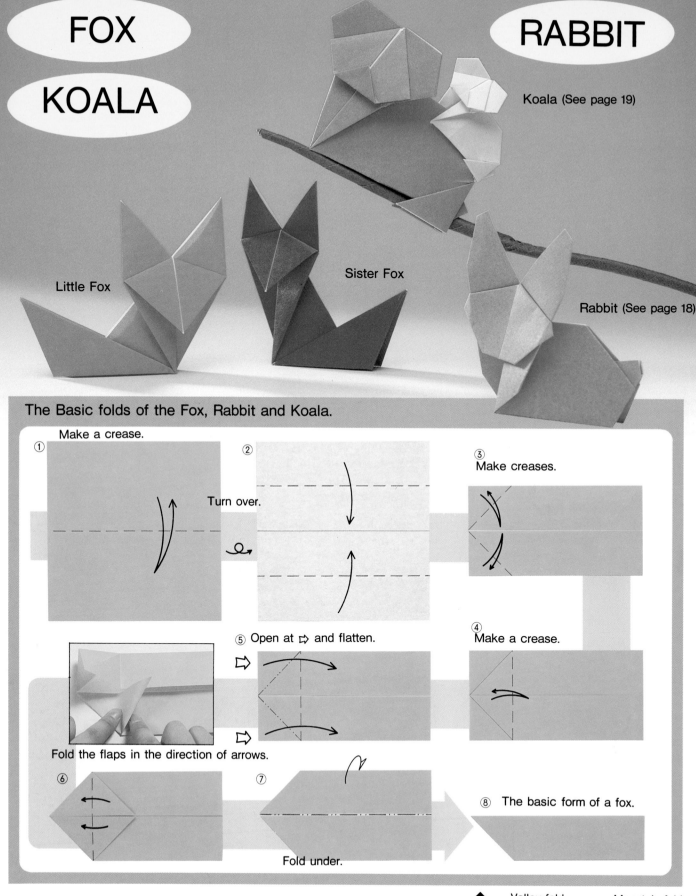

① Make a crease.

② Turn over.

③ Make creases.

④ Make a crease.

⑤ Open at ⇨ and flatten.

Fold the flaps in the direction of arrows.

⑥

⑦ Fold under.

⑧ The basic form of a fox.

16

◆--- Valley fold   —·— Mountain fold

LITTLE FOX

Begin with the basic form on the previous page.

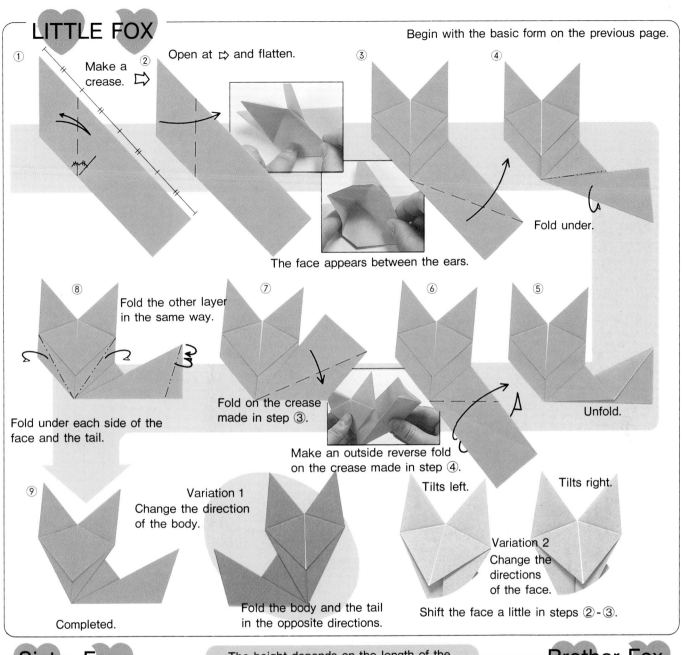

① Make a crease.

② Open at ⇨ and flatten.

The face appears between the ears.

③

④ Fold under.

⑤ Unfold.

Tilts left. Tilts right.

Variation 2 Change the directions of the face.

Shift the face a little in steps ②-③.

⑥

⑦ Fold on the crease made in step ③.

Make an outside reverse fold on the crease made in step ④.

⑧ Fold the other layer in the same way.

Fold under each side of the face and the tail.

⑨ Completed.

Variation 1 Change the direction of the body.

Fold the body and the tail in the opposite directions.

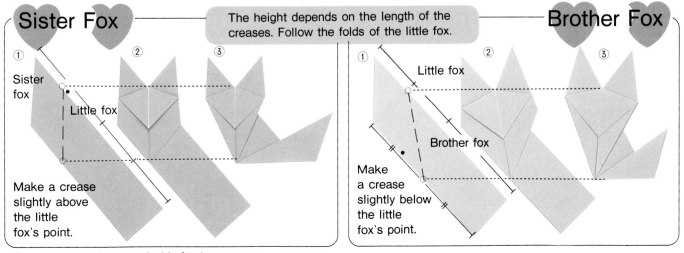

Sister Fox

The height depends on the length of the creases. Follow the folds of the little fox.

Brother Fox

① Sister fox / Little fox

② ③

Make a crease slightly above the little fox's point.

① Little fox / Brother fox

② ③

Make a crease slightly below the little fox's point.

Symbols for folding —— Inside front cover

RABBIT

Begin with step ⑥ of the basic fold on page 16.

① Fold over with the tips of the ears protruding slightly.

②

③ Make a crease.

④ Fold on the center line.

Creases to be made.

⑤ Fold on the crease made in step ③.

⑥

⑦ Pull up as far as possible.

Make an inside reverse fold on crease (a) and pull out (b). (See page 4)

⑧ Open at ▷ and flatten to make the face and ears.

⑨

⑩ Make a crease.

⑪ Unfold.

⑫ b / a / About 1/4.

⑬ Fold inward the tip of the nose and hind legs.

⑭

⑮

⑯ Turn over.

Fold behind.

⑰ Turn over.

Fold the left side in the same way.

Open at ▷ and flatten.

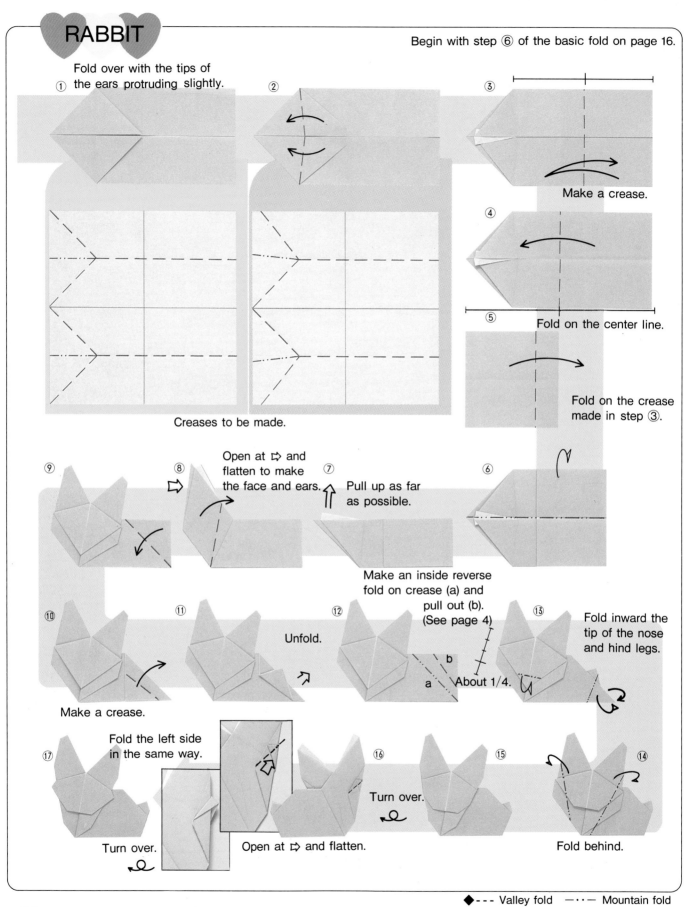

◆--- Valley fold   —·— Mountain fold

KOALA

Begin with step ⑦ of the basic fold on page 16.

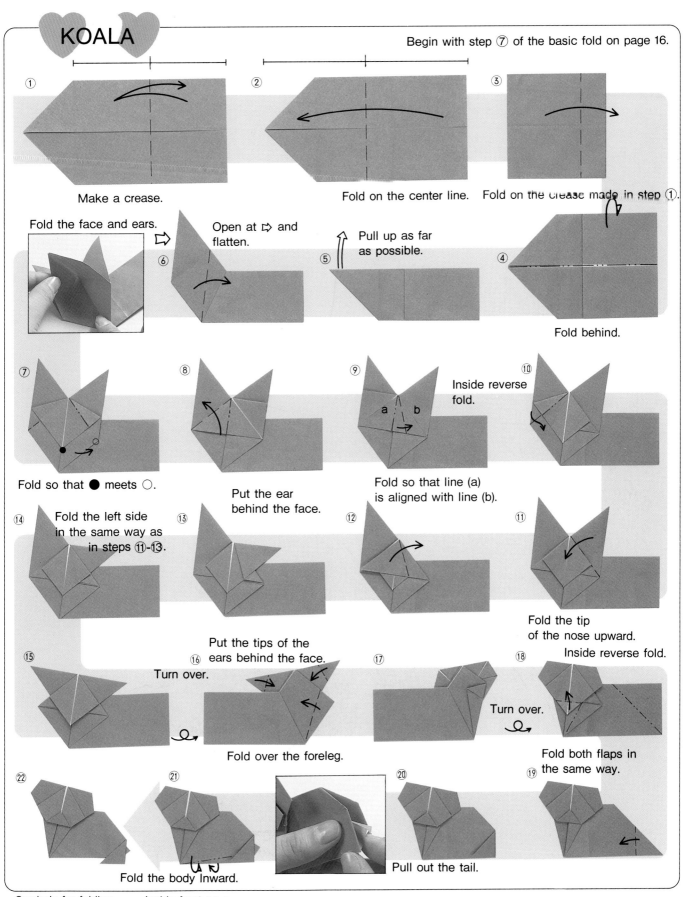

① Make a crease.

② Fold on the center line.

③ Fold on the crease made in step ①.

④ Fold behind.

⑤ Pull up as far as possible.

⑥ Open at ⇨ and flatten.

Fold the face and ears.

⑦ Fold so that ● meets ○.

⑧ Put the ear behind the face.

⑨ Fold so that line (a) is aligned with line (b).

Inside reverse fold.

⑩

⑪ Fold the tip of the nose upward.

⑫

⑬

⑭ Fold the left side in the same way as in steps ⑪-⑬.

⑮ Turn over.

⑯ Put the tips of the ears behind the face.

Fold over the foreleg.

⑰ Turn over.

⑱ Inside reverse fold.

⑲ Fold both flaps in the same way.

⑳ Pull out the tail.

㉑ Fold the body inward.

㉒

Symbols for folding —— Inside front cover

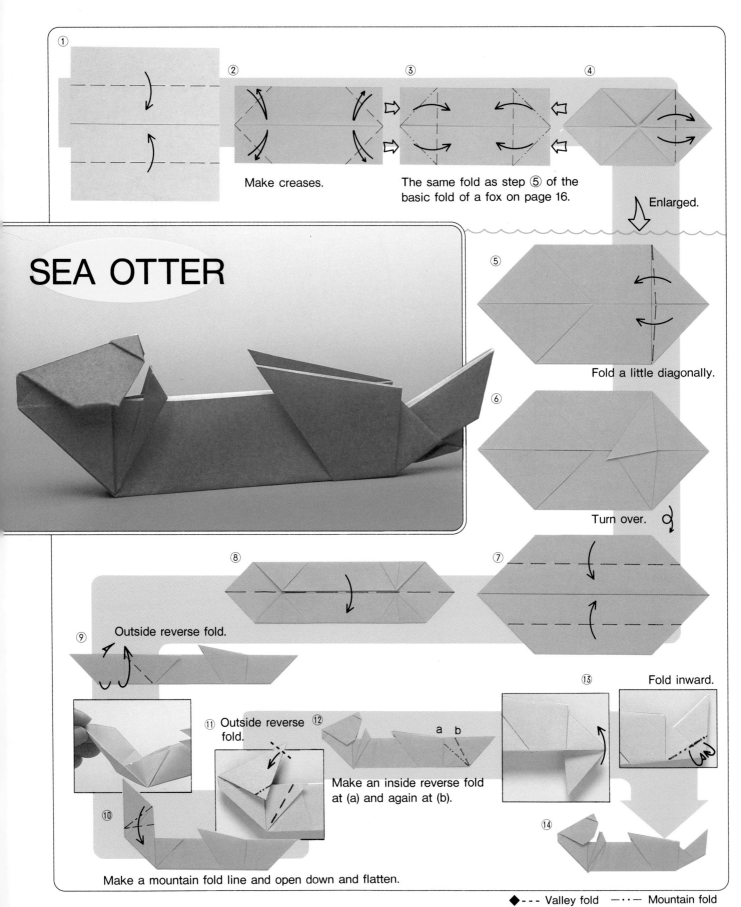

①

② Make creases.

③ The same fold as step ⑤ of the basic fold of a fox on page 16.

④

Enlarged.

SEA OTTER

⑤ Fold a little diagonally.

⑥ Turn over.

⑦

⑧ Outside reverse fold.

⑨

⑩ Make a mountain fold line and open down and flatten.

⑪ Outside reverse fold.

⑫ Make an inside reverse fold at (a) and again at (b).

a b

⑬ Fold inward.

⑭

◆--- Valley fold   —··— Mountain fold

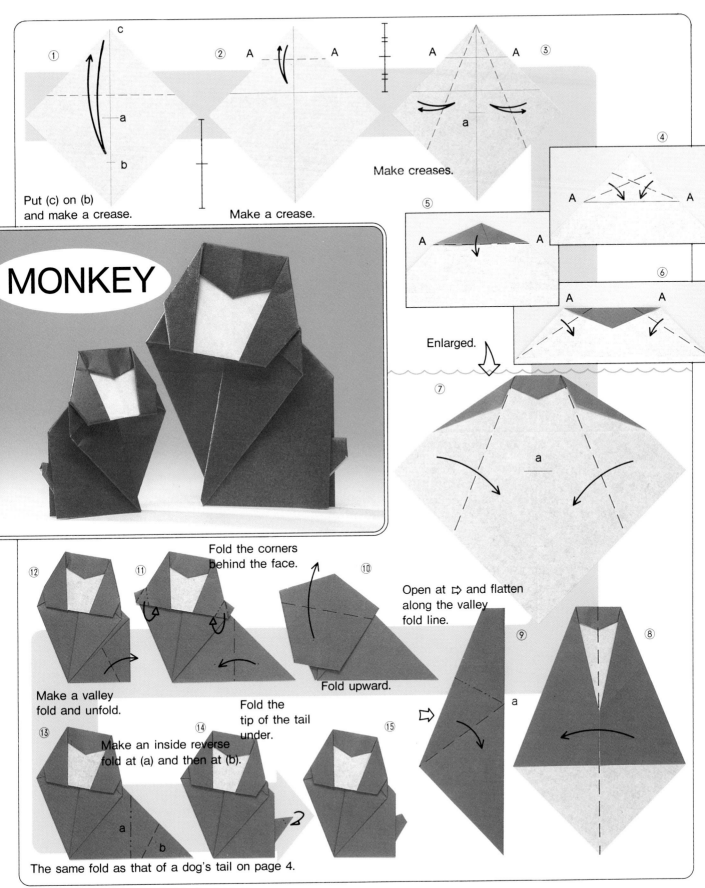

① Put (c) on (b) and make a crease.

② Make a crease.

③ Make creases.

④

⑤

⑥

Enlarged.

⑦

MONKEY

⑧

⑨ Open at ⇨ and flatten along the valley fold line.

⑩ Fold upward.

Fold the corners behind the face.

⑪

⑫ Make a valley fold and unfold.

⑬ Make an inside reverse fold at (a) and then at (b).

Fold the tip of the tail under.

⑭

⑮

The same fold as that of a dog's tail on page 4.

ELEPHANT

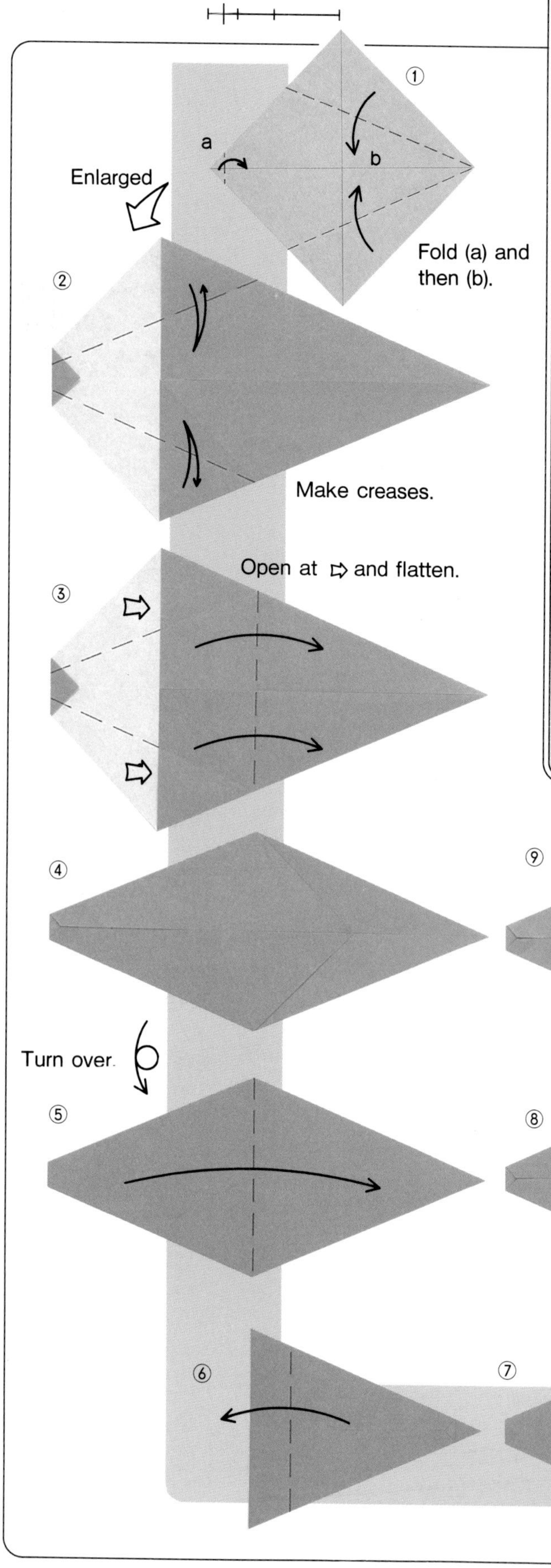

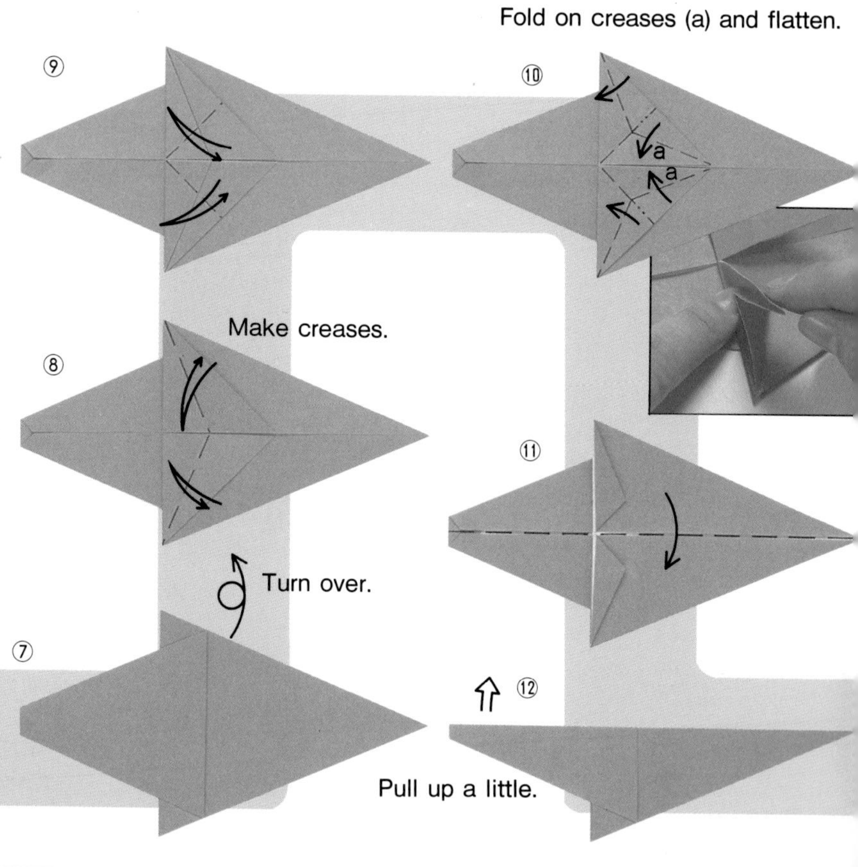

① Fold (a) and then (b).

Enlarged

② Make creases.

③ Open at ⇨ and flatten.

④

Turn over.

⑤

⑥

⑦

⑧ Make creases.

Turn over.

⑨ Fold on creases (a) and flatten.

⑩

⑪

⑫ Pull up a little.

◆--- Valley fold —·— Mountain fold

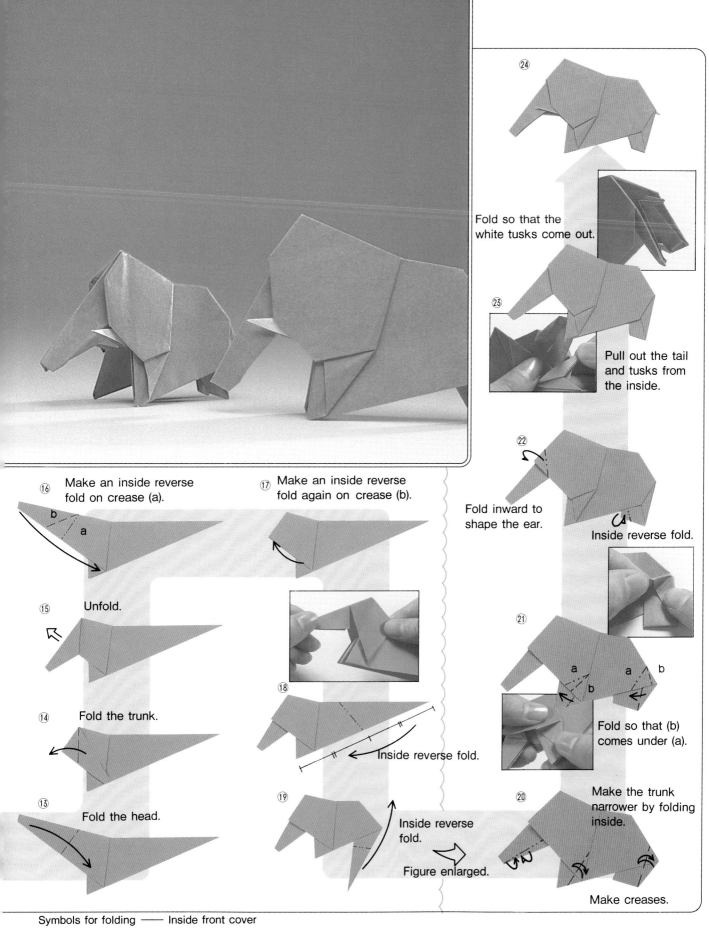

㉔

Fold so that the white tusks come out.

㉓ Pull out the tail and tusks from the inside.

㉒ Fold inward to shape the ear.

Inside reverse fold.

㉑ Fold so that (b) comes under (a).

⑳ Make the trunk narrower by folding inside.

Make creases.

⑯ Make an inside reverse fold on crease (a).

⑰ Make an inside reverse fold again on crease (b).

⑱ Inside reverse fold.

⑲ Inside reverse fold.

Figure enlarged.

⑮ Unfold.

⑭ Fold the trunk.

⑬ Fold the head.

Symbols for folding —— Inside front cover

23

SNAKE

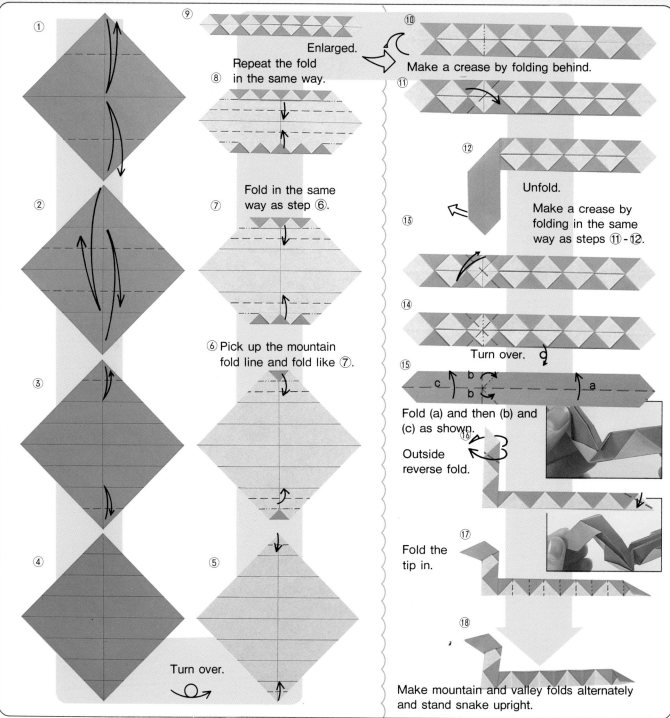

① ② ③ ④

Turn over.

⑤

⑥ Pick up the mountain fold line and fold like ⑦.

⑦ Fold in the same way as step ⑥.

⑧ Fold in the same way.

Repeat the fold in the same way.

⑨ Enlarged.

⑩ Make a crease by folding behind.

⑪

⑫ Unfold.

Make a crease by folding in the same way as steps ⑪ - ⑫.

⑬

⑭ Turn over.

⑮
c   b   b   a

Fold (a) and then (b) and (c) as shown.

Outside reverse fold.

⑯

Fold the tip in.

⑰

⑱

Make mountain and valley folds alternately and stand snake upright.

◆--- Valley fold   —·— Mountain fold   Symbols for folding   —— Inside front cover

2
BIRDS

SEASON'S GREETINGS

FOWLS & CHICKENS

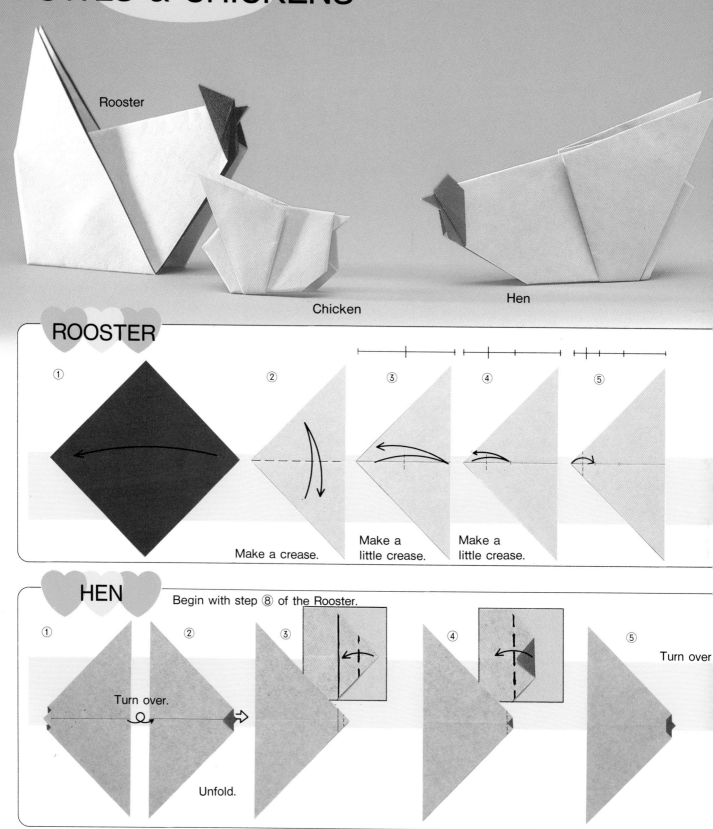

Rooster

Chicken

Hen

ROOSTER

① ② ③ ④ ⑤

Make a crease.

Make a little crease.

Make a little crease.

HEN

Begin with step ⑧ of the Rooster.

① ② ③ ④ ⑤

Turn over.

Unfold.

Turn over

◆--- Valley fold —·— Mountain fold

CHICKEN

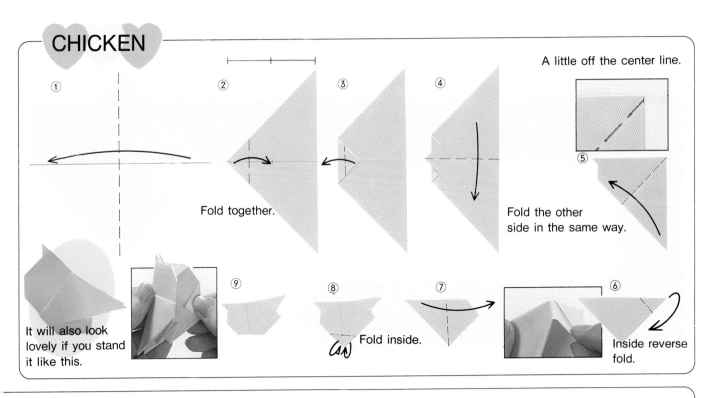

①

② Fold together.

③

④ Fold the other side in the same way.

A little off the center line.

⑤

⑥ Inside reverse fold.

⑦

⑧ Fold inside.

⑨

It will also look lovely if you stand it like this.

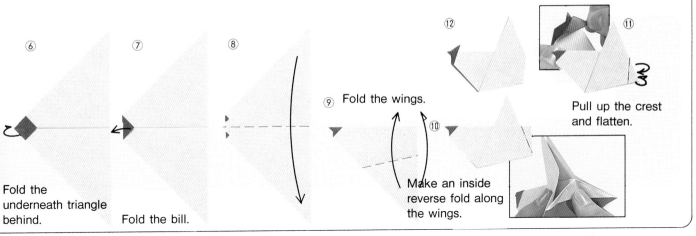

⑥ Fold the underneath triangle behind.

⑦ Fold the bill.

⑧

⑨ Fold the wings.

⑩ Make an inside reverse fold along the wings.

⑪ Pull up the crest and flatten.

⑫

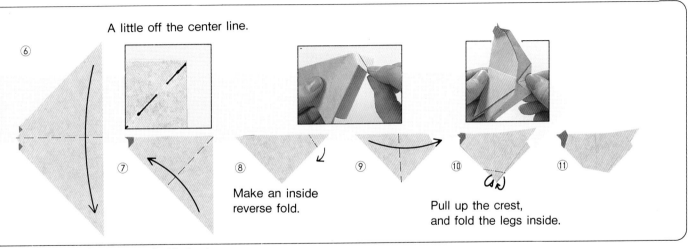

A little off the center line.

⑥

⑦

⑧ Make an inside reverse fold.

⑨

⑩ Pull up the crest, and fold the legs inside.

⑪

Symbols for folding —— Inside front cover

LITTLE BIRDS

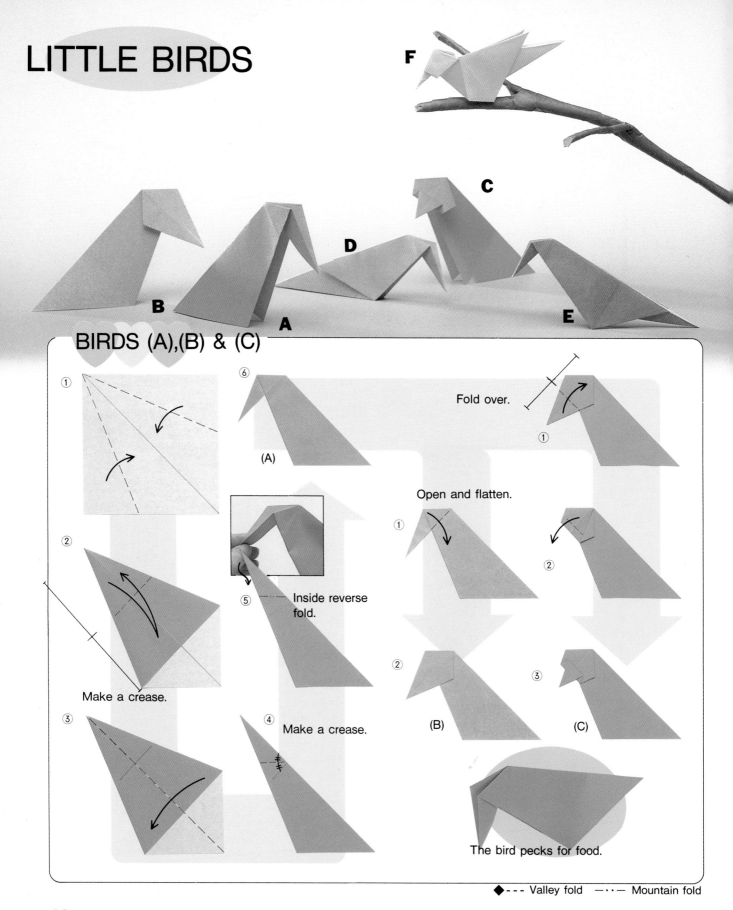

BIRDS (A), (B) & (C)

①

② Make a crease.

③

④ Make a crease.

⑤ —·—·— Inside reverse fold.

⑥

(A)

Fold over.

①

Open and flatten.

①

②

②

(B)

③

(C)

The bird pecks for food.

◆--- Valley fold   —·— Mountain fold

BIRD (D)

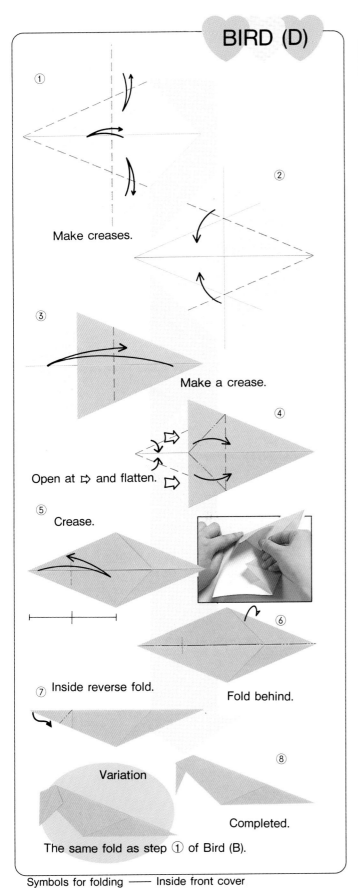

① Make creases.

②

③ Make a crease.

④ Open at ⇨ and flatten.

⑤ Crease.

⑥ Fold behind.

⑦ Inside reverse fold.

⑧ Completed.

Variation

The same fold as step ① of Bird (B).

Symbols for folding ——— Inside front cover

BIRD (E)

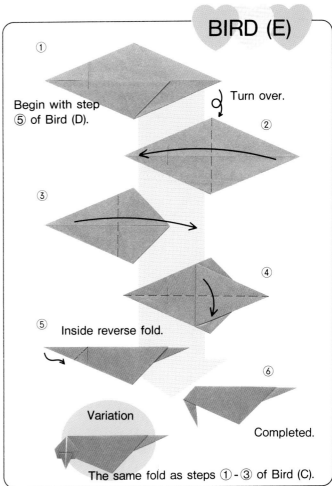

① Begin with step ⑤ of Bird (D). Turn over.

②

③

④

⑤ Inside reverse fold.

⑥ Completed.

Variation

The same fold as steps ①-③ of Bird (C).

BIRD (F)

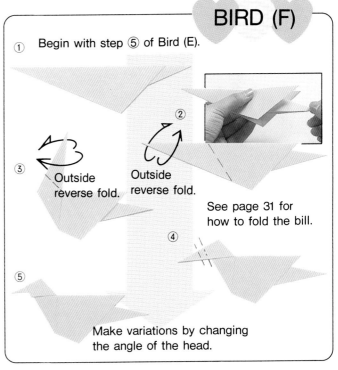

① Begin with step ⑤ of Bird (E).

② Outside reverse fold.

③ Outside reverse fold.

See page 31 for how to fold the bill.

④

⑤ Make variations by changing the angle of the head.

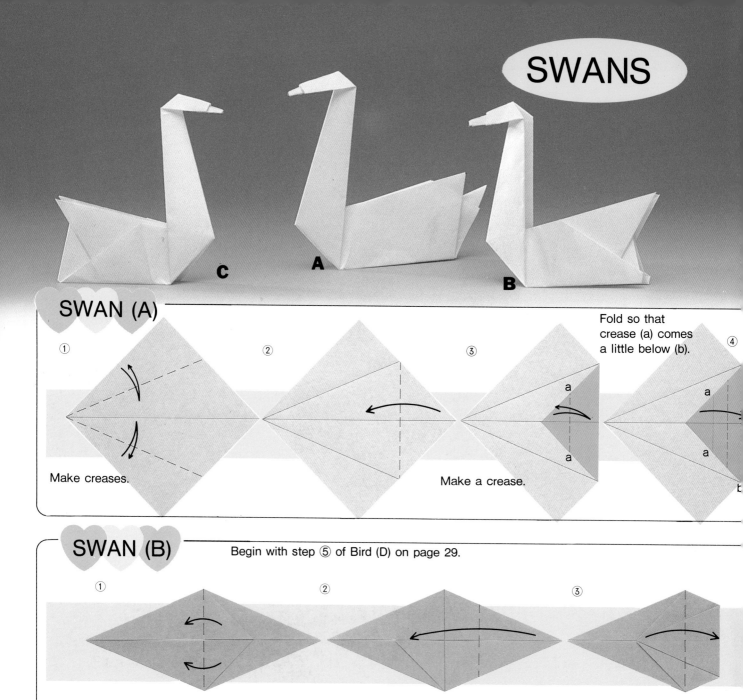

SWANS

C   **A**   **B**

SWAN (A)

Fold so that crease (a) comes a little below (b).

① Make creases.

②

③ Make a crease.

④

a
a

a
a

b

SWAN (B)

Begin with step ⑤ of Bird (D) on page 29.

①

②

③

SWAN (C)

Begin with step ⑤ of Bird (D) on page 29.

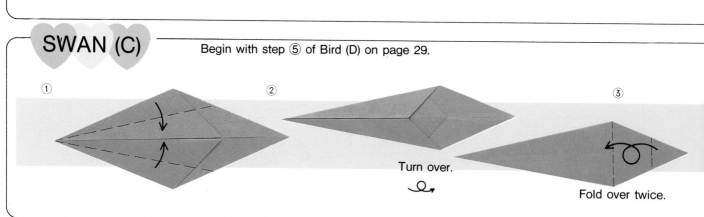

①

②   Turn over.

③   Fold over twice.

◆--- Valley fold   —··— Mountain fold

How to fold the bill
This applies to almost all bills.

① a / b

② Unfold ① and bring (b) to (a).

③ Fold behind on the crease.

④ Fold again on the creases.

⑤

Fold the bill as shown above.

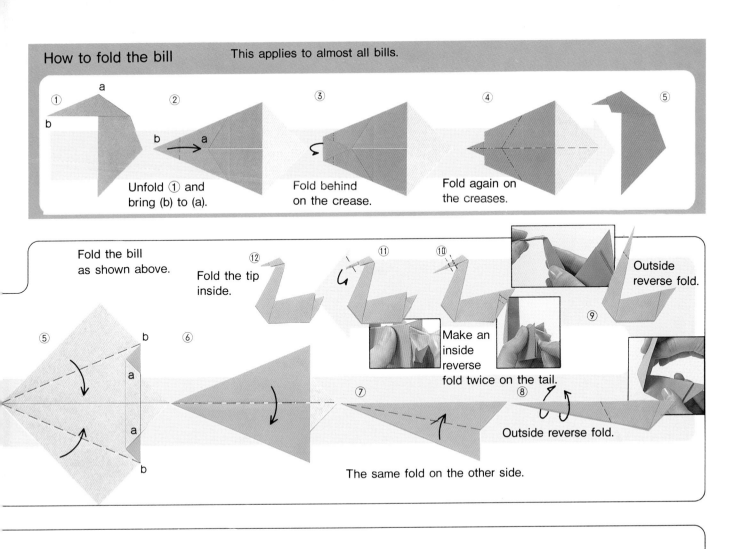

⑤ b a a b

⑥

⑦ The same fold on the other side.

⑧ Outside reverse fold.

⑨ Outside reverse fold.

⑩ Make an inside reverse fold twice on the tail.

⑪

⑫ Fold the tip inside.

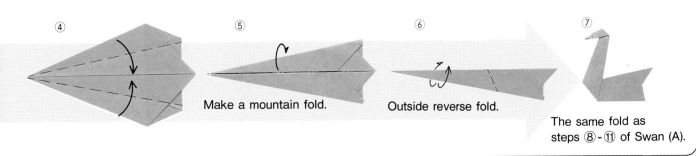

④ Make a mountain fold.

⑤ Outside reverse fold.

⑥

⑦ The same fold as steps ⑧-⑪ of Swan (A).

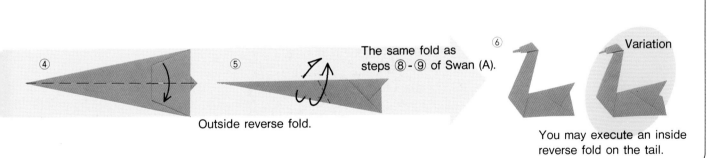

④

⑤ Outside reverse fold.

The same fold as steps ⑧-⑨ of Swan (A).

⑥ You may execute an inside reverse fold on the tail.

Variation

Symbols for folding —— Inside front cover

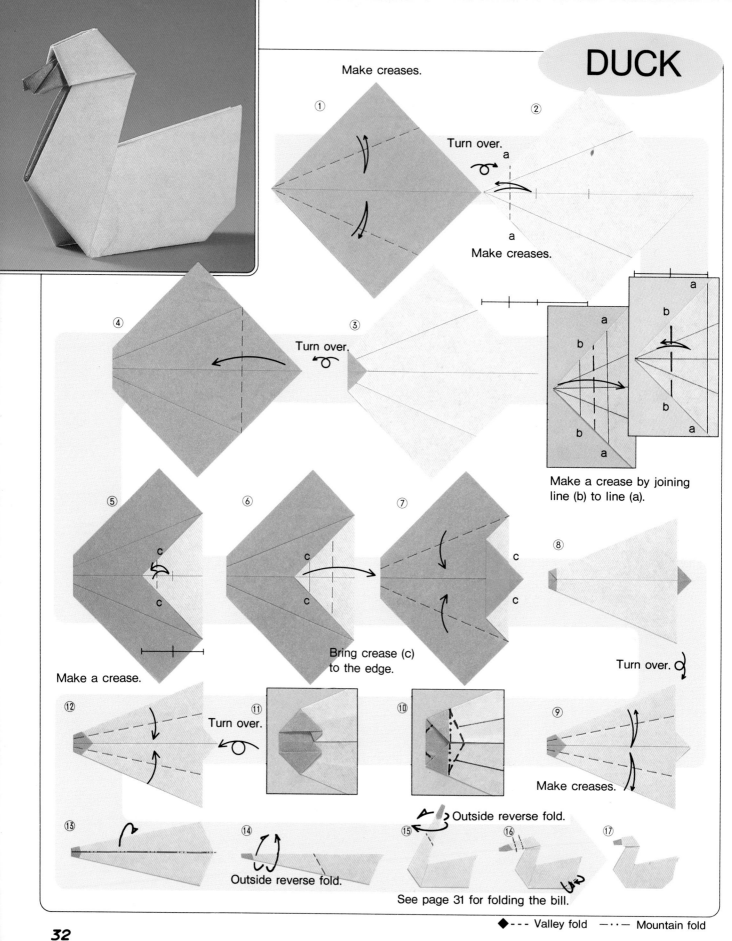

DUCK

Make creases.

① Make creases.

② Turn over.
a
a
Make creases.

Make a crease by joining line (b) to line (a).

④ Turn over.

③

⑤ Make a crease.

⑥ Bring crease (c) to the edge.

⑦

⑧ Turn over.

⑫

⑪ Turn over.

⑩

⑨ Make creases.

Outside reverse fold.

⑬

⑭ Outside reverse fold.

⑮

⑯

⑰

See page 31 for folding the bill.

◆--- Valley fold   —·—·— Mountain fold

32

SPARROW

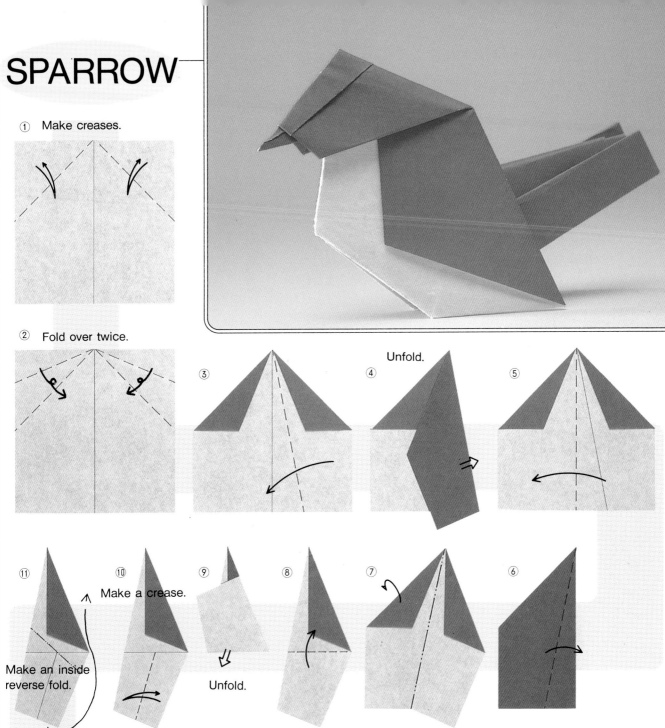

① Make creases.

② Fold over twice.

③

④ Unfold.

⑤

⑥

⑦

⑧

⑨ Unfold.

⑩ Make a crease.

⑪ Make an inside reverse fold.

Fold this part inside the wing.

⑫

⑬

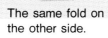

The same fold on the other side.

⑭ Fold over and insert the tip in between the wing.

⑮

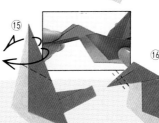

Outside reverse fold.

⑯

See page 31 for folding the bill.

⑰

Symbols for folding —— Inside front cover

PEACOCK

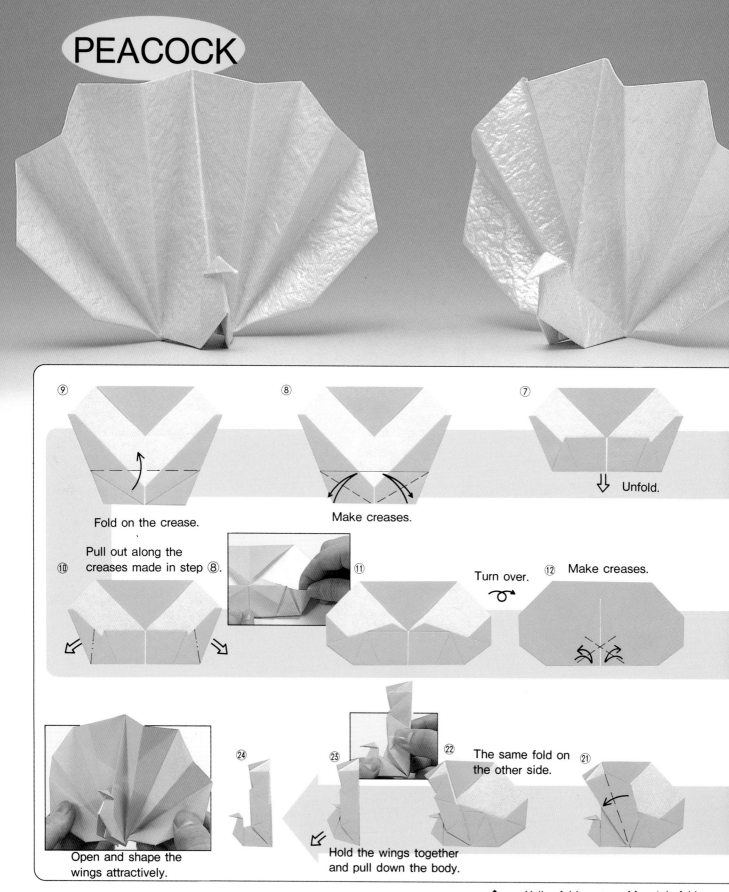

⑨ Fold on the crease.

⑧ Make creases.

⑦ Unfold.

⑩ Pull out along the creases made in step ⑧.

⑪

⑫ Turn over. Make creases.

㉔ Open and shape the wings attractively.

㉓ Hold the wings together and pull down the body.

㉒

㉑ The same fold on the other side.

◆--- Valley fold   —·— Mountain fold

Make creases.

①

②

③ Fold over on the crease.

④ Make a crease.

⑤ Fold by joining crease (a) to line (b).

a — a

b — b

⑥ Fold behind.

b a — a b

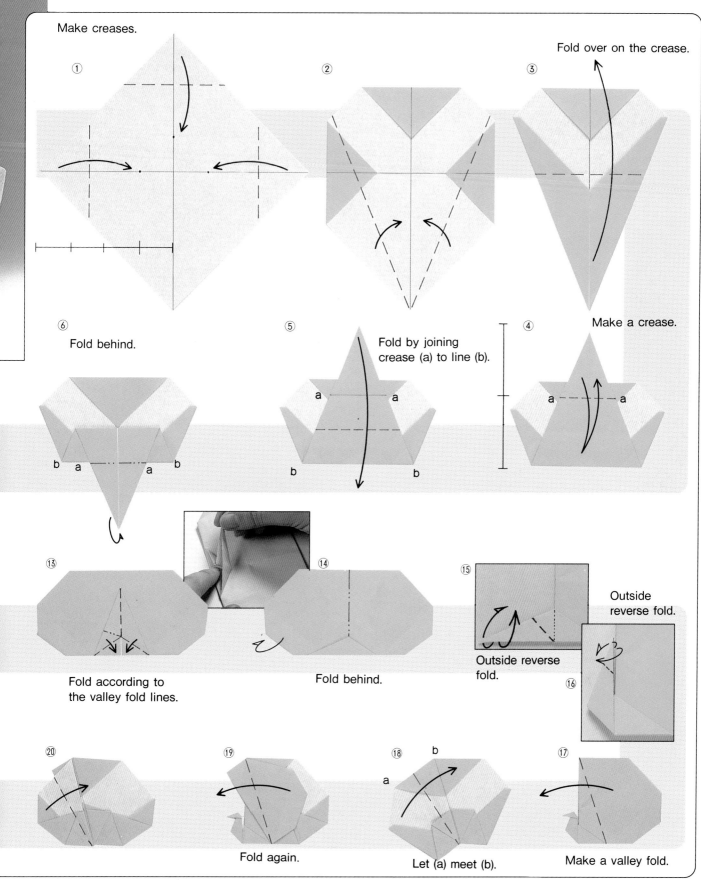

⑬ Fold according to the valley fold lines.

⑭ Fold behind.

⑮ Outside reverse fold.

Outside reverse fold.

⑯

⑰ Make a valley fold.

⑱ a b — Let (a) meet (b).

⑲ Fold again.

⑳

WALKING SPOT-BILLED DUCKS

WALKING SPOT-BILLED DUCK

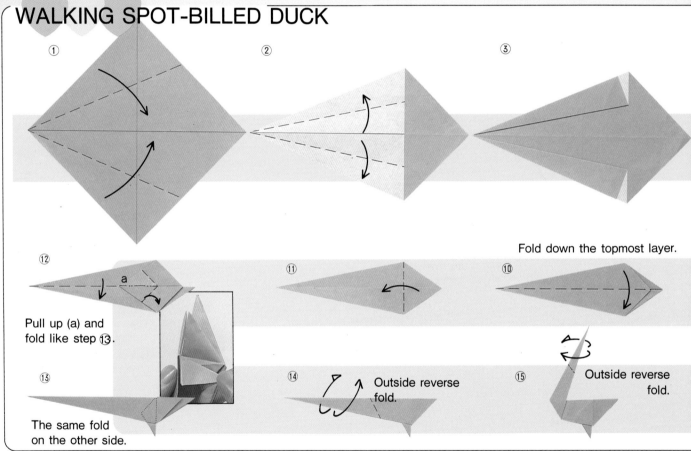

① ② ③

Fold down the topmost layer.

⑫ ⑪ ⑩

a

Pull up (a) and
fold like step ⑬.

⑬

The same fold
on the other side.

⑭ Outside reverse
fold.

⑮ Outside reverse
fold.

SWIMMING SPOT-BILLED DUCK

Begin with step ② above.

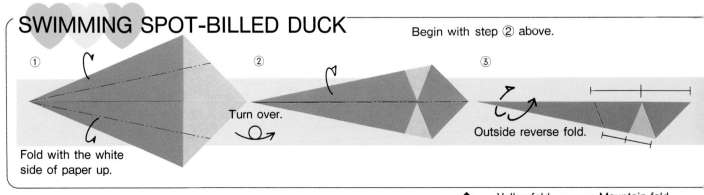

① ② ③

Turn over.

Outside reverse fold.

Fold with the white
side of paper up.

◆--- Valley fold   —·— Mountain fold

SWIMMING SPOT-BILLED DUCKS

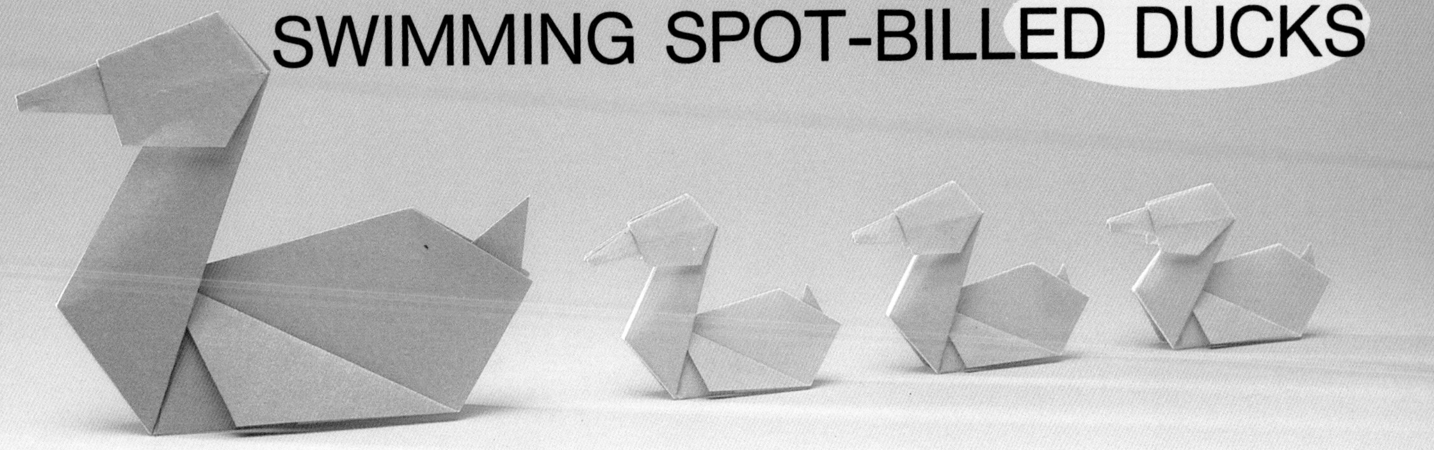

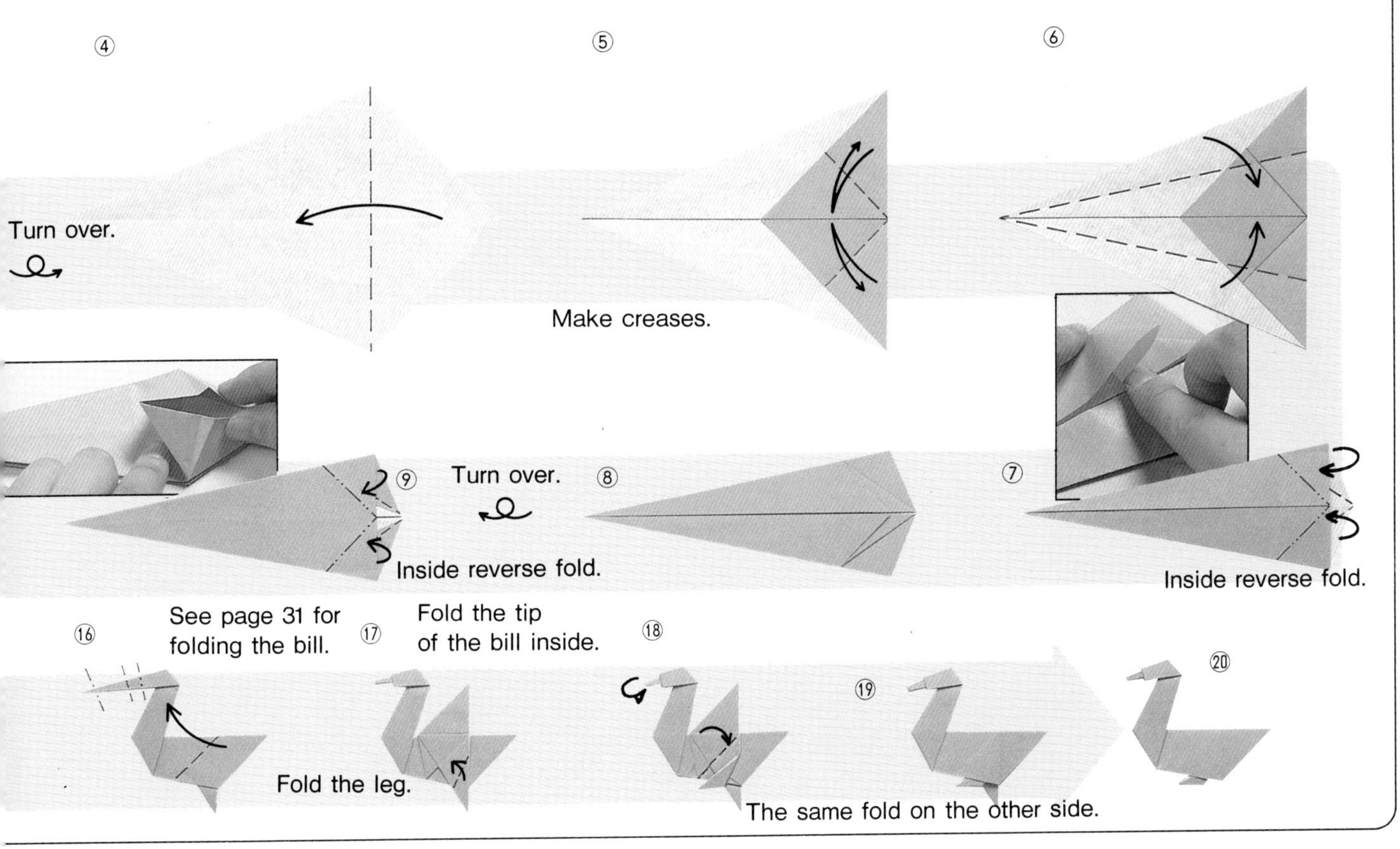
④
Turn over.
⑤
Make creases.
⑥
⑦
Inside reverse fold.
⑧
Turn over.
⑨
Inside reverse fold.
⑯
See page 31 for
folding the bill.
Fold the leg.
⑰
Fold the tip
of the bill inside.
⑱
⑲
The same fold on the other side.
⑳

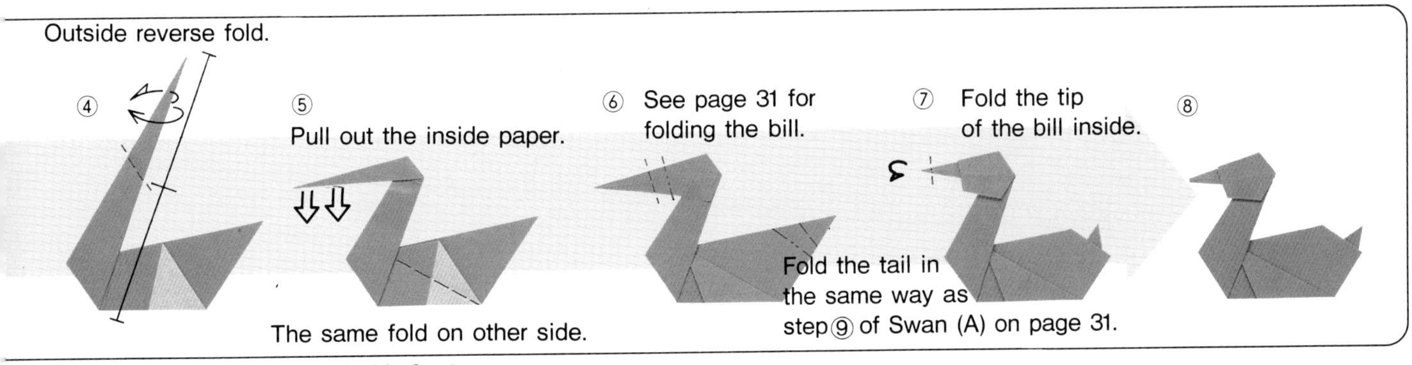
Outside reverse fold.
④
⑤
Pull out the inside paper.
The same fold on other side.
⑥
See page 31 for
folding the bill.
Fold the tail in
the same way as
step ⑨ of Swan (A) on page 31.
⑦
Fold the tip
of the bill inside.
⑧

Symbols for folding —— Inside front cover

PENGUINS

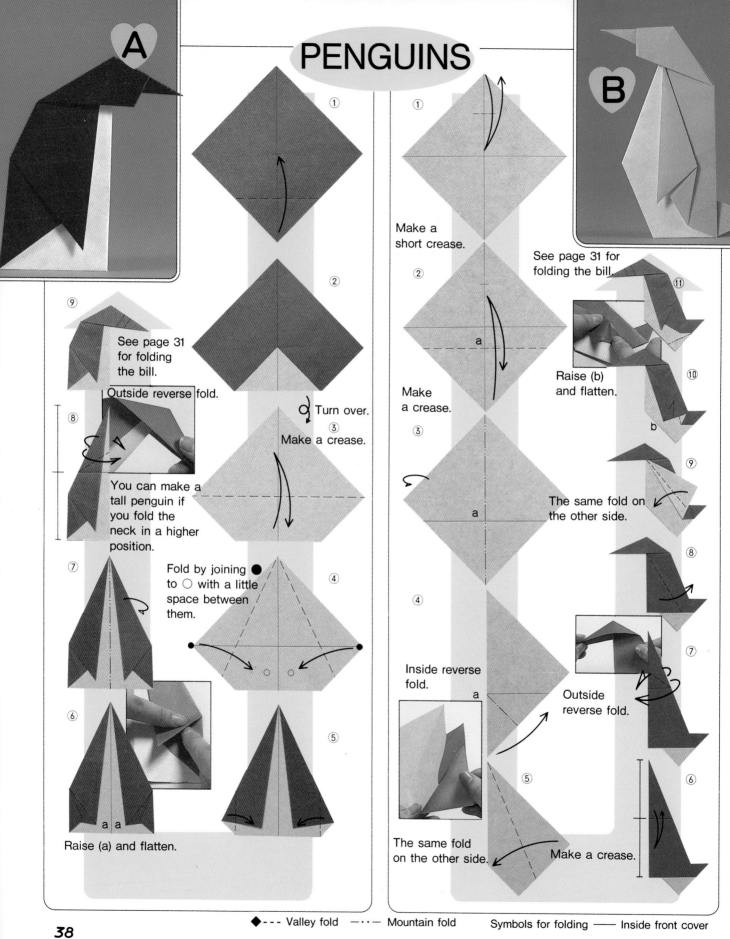

A

①

②

Turn over.
Make a crease.
③

Fold by joining ● to ○ with a little space between them.
④

⑤

⑥

Raise (a) and flatten.

a a

⑦

⑧

Outside reverse fold.

You can make a tall penguin if you fold the neck in a higher position.

⑨

See page 31 for folding the bill.

B

①

Make a short crease.

②

a

Make a crease.

③

a

④

Inside reverse fold.

a

The same fold on the other side.

⑤

Make a crease.

⑥

⑦

Outside reverse fold.

⑧

⑨

The same fold on the other side.

⑩

b

Raise (b) and flatten.

⑪

See page 31 for folding the bill.

◆--- Valley fold   —·—· Mountain fold   Symbols for folding —— Inside front cover

3
FISH, INSECTS, FLOWERS

GOLDFISH

Begin with step ⑥ of the Fox on page 16.

① Make creases.

Make valley folds.

②

③

④ Fold behind.

⑤ Make three creases and make an inside reverse fold on crease (a).

a   b   c

a   b   c

⑥ Make an inside reverse fold on crease (b).

⑦ Make an inside reverse fold on crease (c).

c

Fold inward. Make a crease.

⑨ Fold (a) under (b). (Inside reverse fold).

b
a

⑩

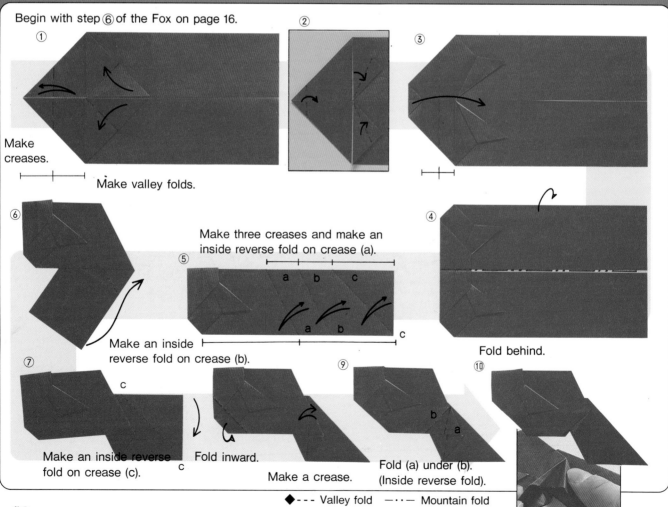

◆--- Valley fold   —·— Mountain fold

MOBILE FRAME

This frame can be used to display the goldfish.

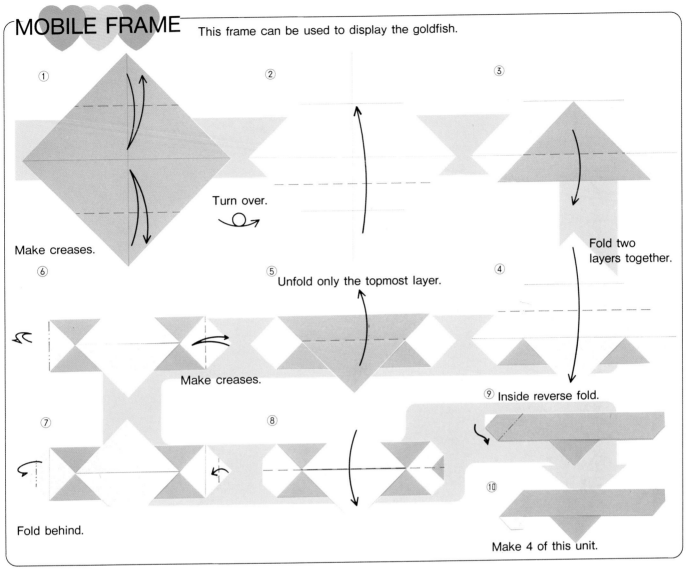

① Make creases.

② Turn over.

③ Fold two layers together.

④

⑤ Unfold only the topmost layer.

⑥ Make creases.

⑦ Fold behind.

⑧

⑨ Inside reverse fold.

⑩ Make 4 of this unit.

HOW TO ASSEMBLE

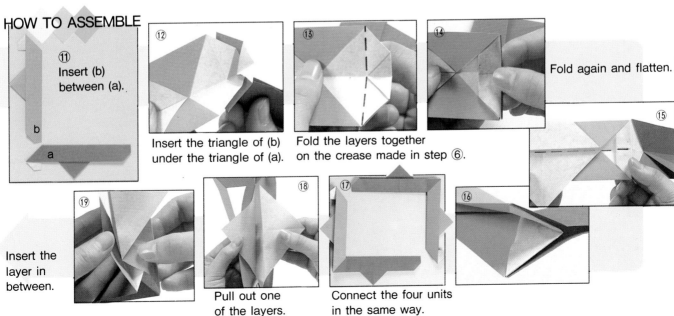

⑪ Insert (b) between (a).

b
a

⑫ Insert the triangle of (b) under the triangle of (a).

⑬ Fold the layers together on the crease made in step ⑥.

⑭ Fold again and flatten.

⑮

⑯

⑰ Connect the four units in the same way.

⑱ Pull out one of the layers.

⑲ Insert the layer in between.

Symbols for folding —— Inside front cover

FROGS

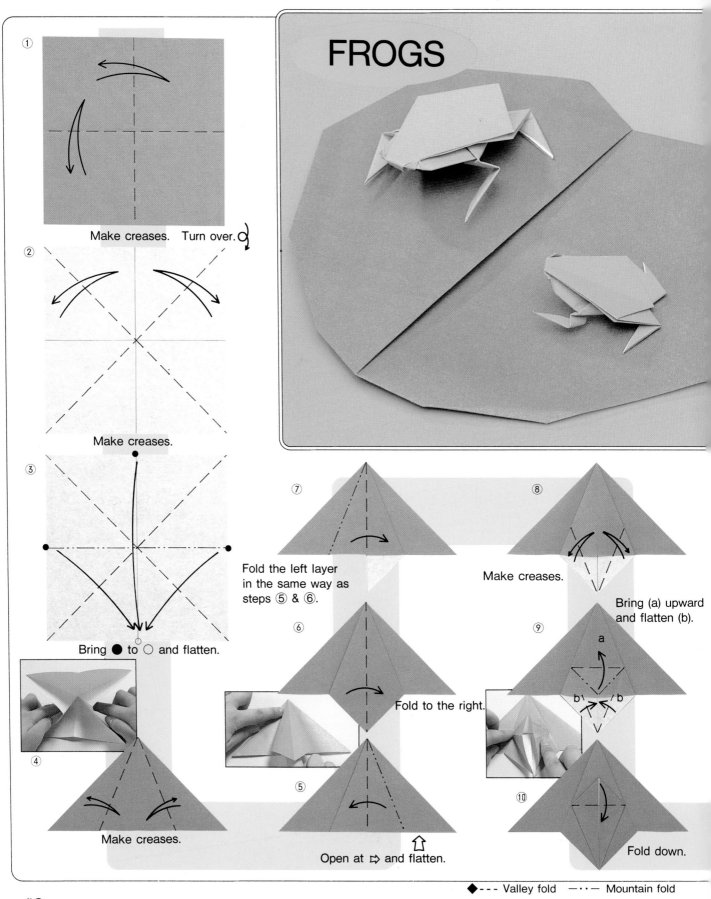

① Make creases. Turn over.

② Make creases.

③ Bring ● to ○ and flatten.

④ Make creases.

⑤ Open at ⇨ and flatten.

⑥ Fold to the right.

⑦ Fold the left layer in the same way as steps ⑤ & ⑥.

⑧ Make creases.

⑨ Bring (a) upward and flatten (b).

a

b b

⑩ Fold down.

◆--- Valley fold   —··— Mountain fold

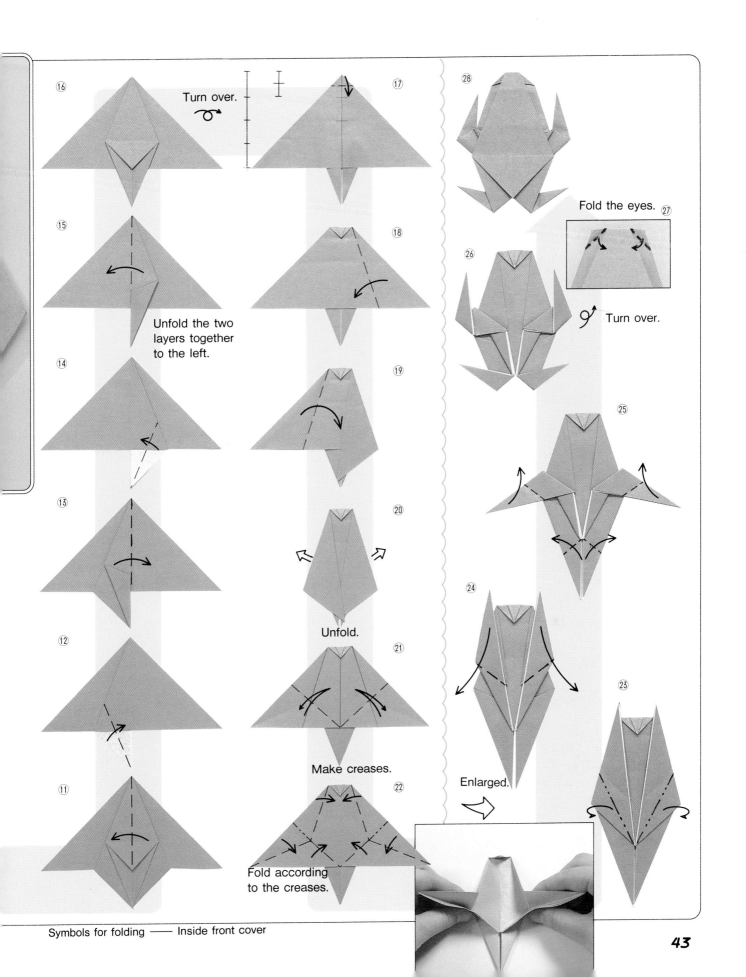

⑯ Turn over.

⑰

⑮ Unfold the two layers together to the left.

⑱

⑭

⑲

⑬

⑳ Unfold.

⑫

㉑ Make creases.

⑪

㉒ Fold according to the creases.

㉘

Fold the eyes. ㉗

㉖ Turn over.

㉕

㉔ Enlarged.

㉓

Symbols for folding —— Inside front cover

43

BUTTERFLIES (A)&(B)

Begin with the Catamaran on page 45.

①

Bring the topmost layer to the left.

②

Bring down and flatten.

③

Fold the left layers in the same way as steps ①-②.

④

Fold the topmost layer on the crease.

⑤

Fold again.

⑥

Fold the other layer to the left.

⑦

Fold the left layer on the crease.

⑧

Fold again.

BUTTERFLIES

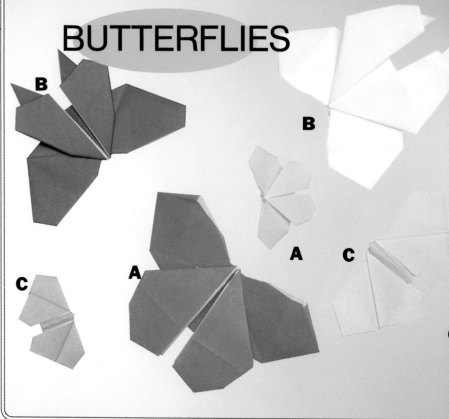

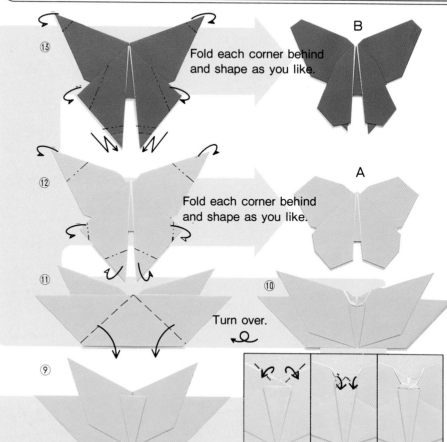

⑬ Fold each corner behind and shape as you like. **B**

⑫ Fold each corner behind and shape as you like. **A**

⑪

⑩ Turn over.

⑨

◆--- Valley fold —·— Mountain fold

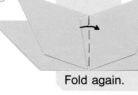

BUTTERFLY (C)

Using a small sheet of paper, you can fold it easily.

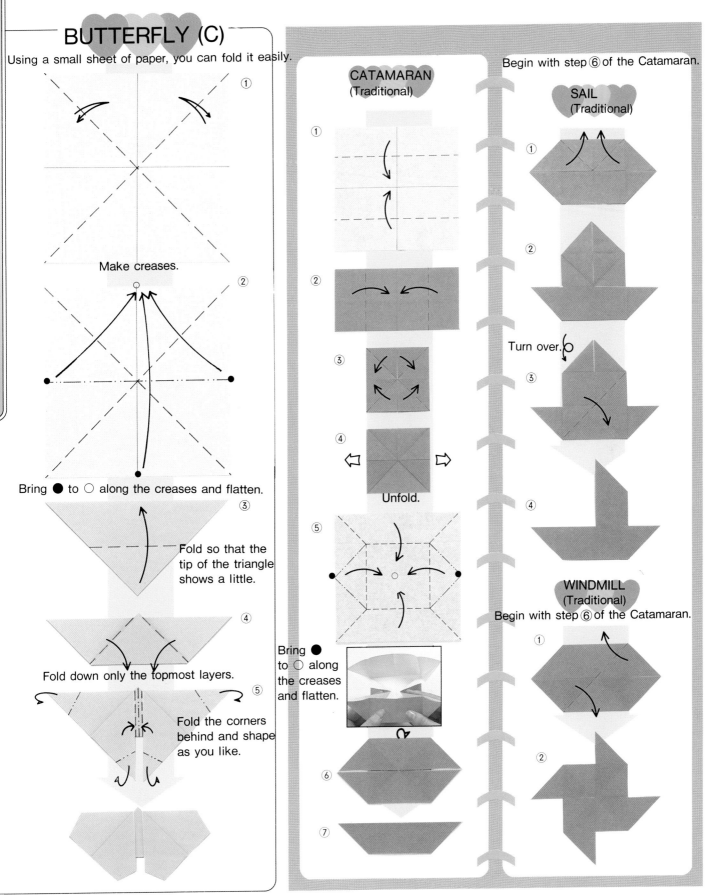

① Make creases.

② Bring ● to ○ along the creases and flatten.

③ Fold so that the tip of the triangle shows a little.

④ Fold down only the topmost layers.

⑤ Fold the corners behind and shape as you like.

CATAMARAN (Traditional)

①
②
③
④ Unfold.
⑤ Bring ● to ○ along the creases and flatten.
⑥
⑦

Begin with step ⑥ of the Catamaran.

SAIL (Traditional)

①
②
Turn over.
③
④

WINDMILL (Traditional)

Begin with step ⑥ of the Catamaran.

①
②

Symbols for folding —— Inside front cover

FLOWER (A) — FLOWER (B)

TULIPS

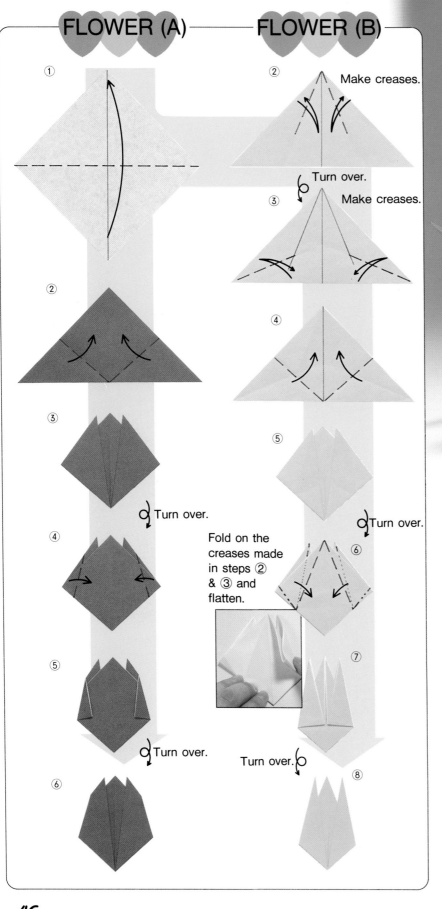

FLOWER (A)

①

②

③

④

⑤

⑥ Turn over.

FLOWER (B)

② Make creases.

Turn over.

③ Make creases.

④

⑤

Turn over.

Fold on the creases made in steps ② & ③ and flatten.

⑥

⑦

Turn over.

⑧

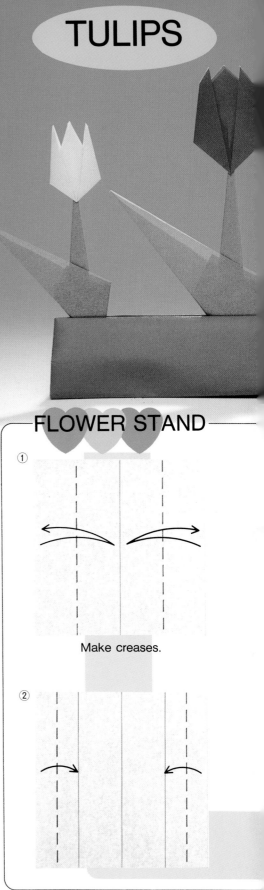

FLOWER STAND

①

Make creases.

②

◆--- Valley fold   —·— Mountain fold

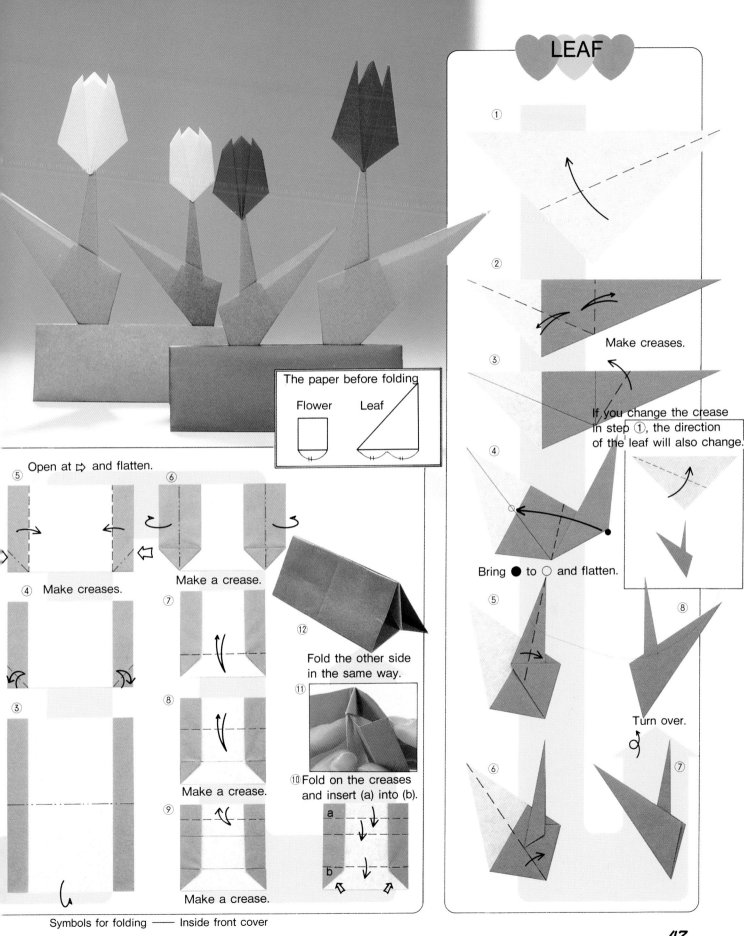

LEAF

①

② Make creases.

③ If you change the crease in step ①, the direction of the leaf will also change.

④ Bring ● to ○ and flatten.

⑤

⑥

⑦

⑧ Turn over.

The paper before folding

Flower   Leaf

Open at ▷ and flatten.

⑤

⑥ Make a crease.

④ Make creases.

③

⑦ Make a crease.

⑧ Make a crease.

⑨ Make a crease.

⑫ Fold the other side in the same way.

⑪

⑩ Fold on the creases and insert (a) into (b).

a

b

Symbols for folding —— Inside front cover

CARNATIONS   IRISES

See page 50 for the Iris.   See page 47 for the flower stand.

CALYX

① ② ③ ④

Fold behind.   Insert into
the stem.

The paper
before folding.
Stem & Leaf   Flower
Calyx

CARNATION

STEM & LEAF

Begin with step ⑤ of the Little Bird (D) on page 29.

① ② ③ ④ ⑤ ⑥

Turn over. | Fold on the
creases about
1/3 from the sides. | Turn over. | | Turn over. | Insert the
calyx into
this stem.

◆--- Valley fold   —·— Mountain fold

48

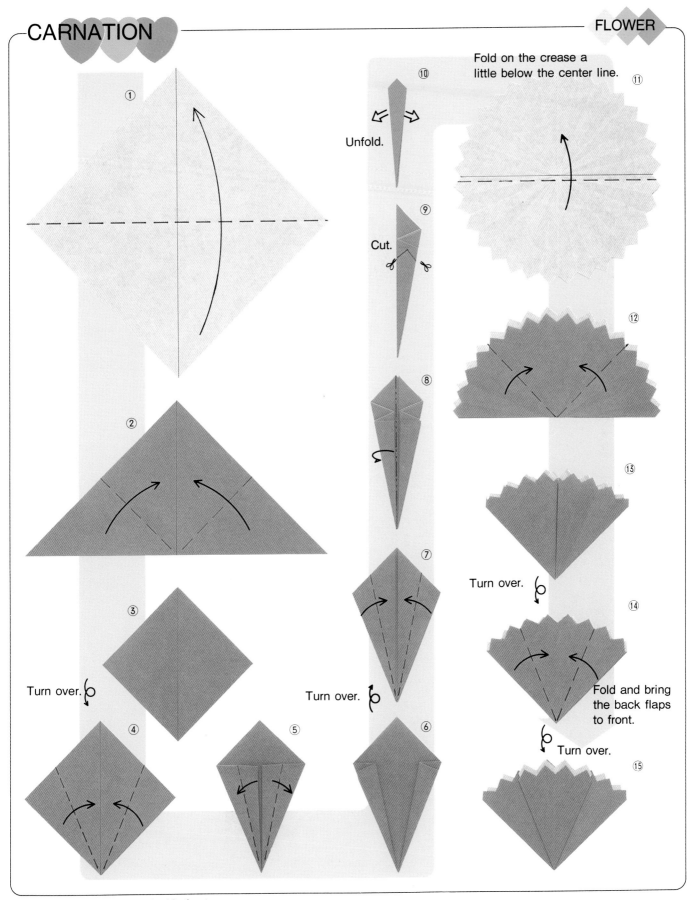

①

②

③ Turn over.

④

⑤

⑥

⑦ Turn over.

⑧

⑨ Cut.

⑩ Unfold.

⑪ Fold on the crease a little below the center line.

⑫

⑬ Turn over.

⑭ Fold and bring the back flaps to front.

Turn over.

⑮

Symbols for folding —— Inside front cover

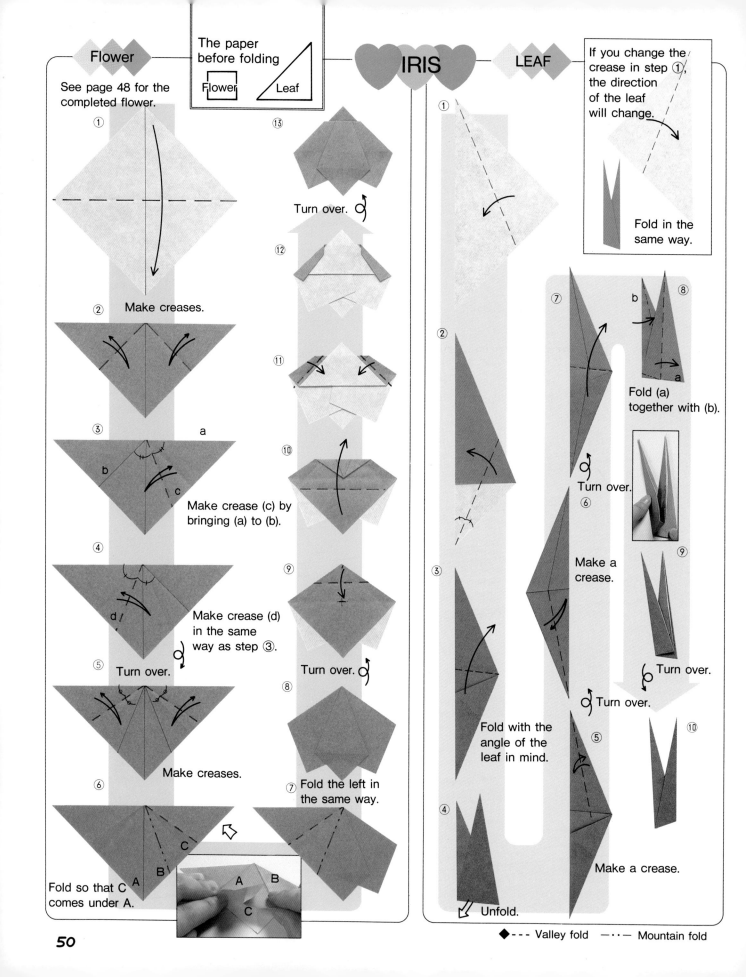

Flower

See page 48 for the completed flower.

The paper before folding

Flower

Leaf

IRIS

LEAF

If you change the crease in step ①, the direction of the leaf will change.

Fold in the same way.

① Make creases.

②

③ a

b

c

Make crease (c) by bringing (a) to (b).

④

d

Make crease (d) in the same way as step ③.

Turn over.

⑤ Turn over.

Make creases.

⑥

Fold so that C comes under A.

A B C

A B

C

⑬ Turn over.

⑫

⑪

⑩

⑨ Turn over.

⑧ Turn over.

⑦ Fold the left in the same way.

①

②

③

Fold with the angle of the leaf in mind.

④

Unfold.

⑤ Make a crease.

Turn over.

⑥ Make a crease.

⑦

⑧ b

a

Fold (a) together with (b).

Turn over.

⑨ Turn over.

⑩

50

◆--- Valley fold   —·— Mountain fold

4

PRACTICAL ORIGAMI

BASIC BOX & VARIATIONS

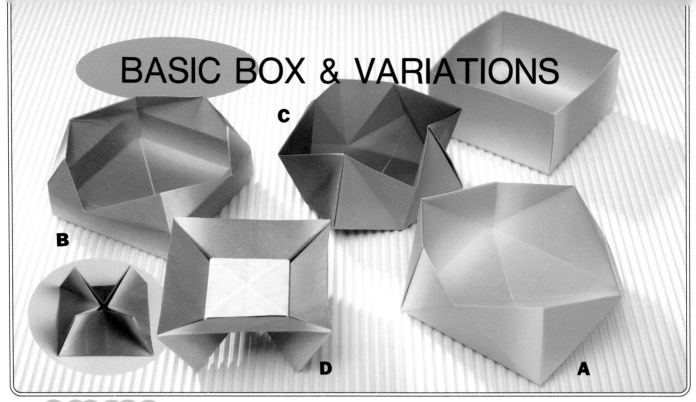

C

B

D

A

BASIC BOX

Make creases clearly.

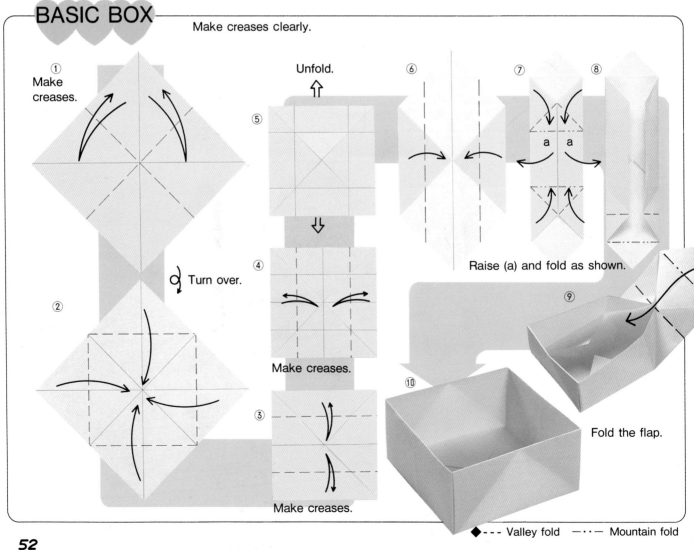

① Make creases.

② Turn over.

③ Make creases.

④ Make creases.

⑤ Unfold.

⑥

⑦ a a

⑧ Raise (a) and fold as shown.

⑨

⑩ Fold the flap.

◆--- Valley fold   —·— Mountain fold

52

Begin with step ⑤ on page 52. Make creases respectively, and make the boxes in the same way.

BOX (A)

①

②

View from the top View from the side

b
a c
d

③

b
c
a
d

Variation

If you fold all the flaps up, you can make the bottom white.

BOX (B)

①

② Turn over.

③ Turn over.

④
b c
a d

View from the top

b
a c
d

View from the side

⑤
b c
a d

BOX (C)

①

② Turn over.

③ Turn over.

④
b c
a d

View from the top

b
a c
d
b

View from the side

⑤
c
a d

BOX (D)

① Fold behind.

② Turn over.

③ Turn over.

④

View from the top

Squeeze the four bottom corners with fingers and fold inward.

⑤

Symbols for folding —— Inside front cover

53

BASIC BOX WITH FLAPS

① Make creases.

Turn over.

②

③

Bring ● to ○ and flatten.

④

Enlarged.

BOX WITH FLAPS & VARIATIONS

A

B

BOX WITH FLAPS

⑥ Turn over. ⑦

Fold in the same way as steps ④–⑥.

⑧

⑤ Open at ▷ and flatten.

⑨

⑫ Fold the flap downwa[rd]

⑪ Make a crease.

⑩ Fold back the flaps.

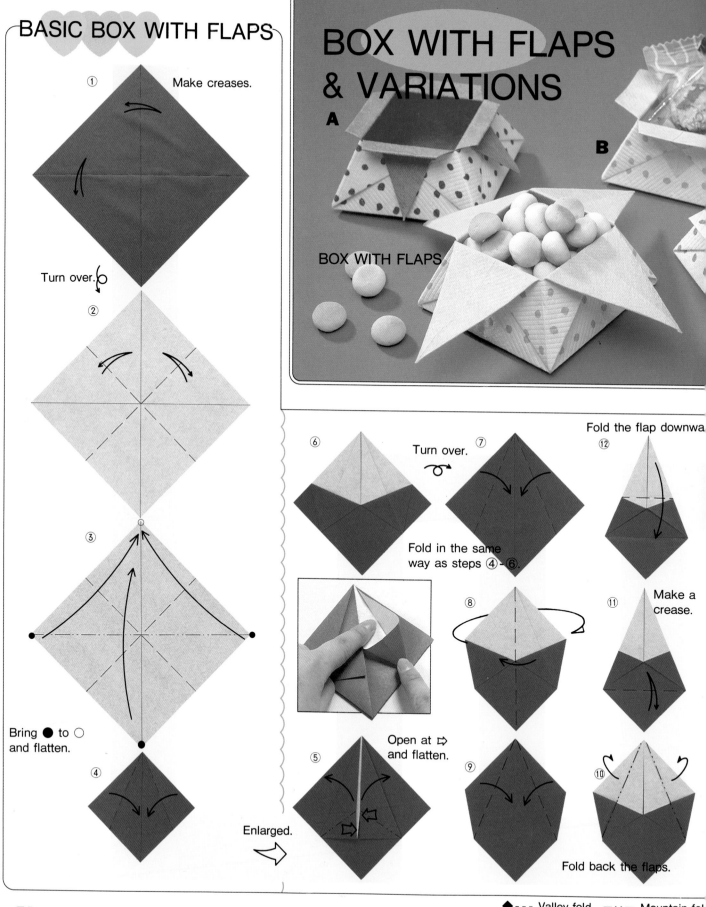

◆--- Valley fold —·— Mountain fol[d]

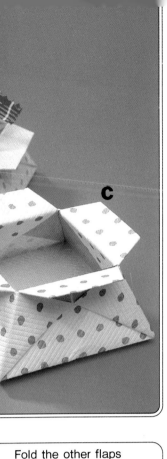

Begin with step ⑫ of the Box with Flaps.

(A) (STAR FLAPS)

①

②

Fold the other flaps in the same way and open.

③

④

⑥

(B) (WHITE FLAPS)

① Unfold.

② a a

Fold on crease (a).

③ a a

④

⑤

Fold the other flaps in the same way and open.

(C) (COLORED FLAPS)

Begin with step ③ of (B).

Unfold.

①

②

③

④

⑤

Fold the other flaps in the same way and open.

⑥

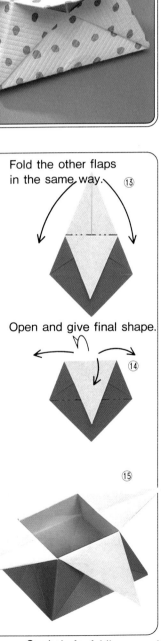

Fold the other flaps in the same way. ⑬

Open and give final shape.

⑭

⑮

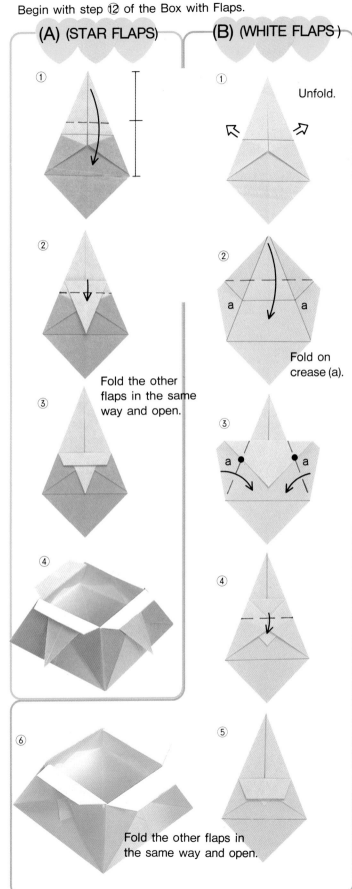

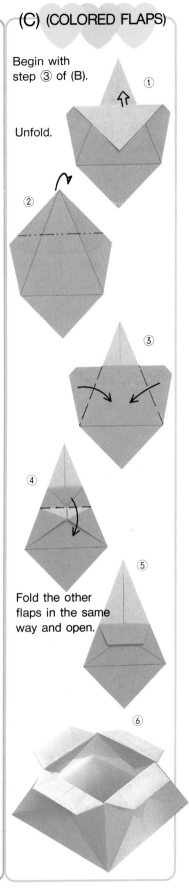

BOXES WITH HANDLES

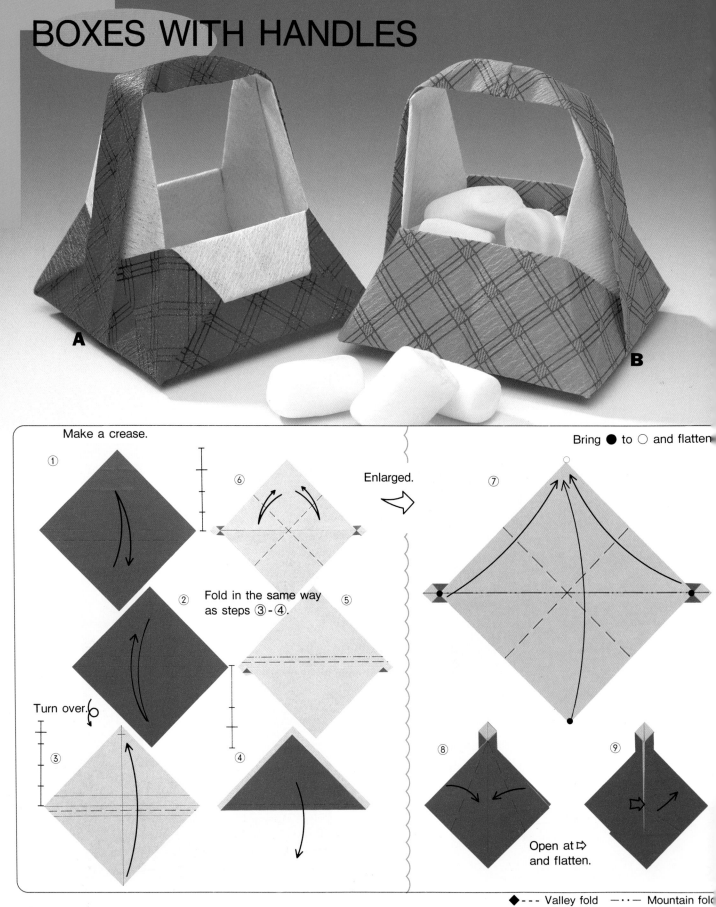

A

B

Make a crease.

①

⑥

Enlarged.

Bring ● to ○ and flatten

⑦

② Fold in the same way as steps ③-④.

⑤

Turn over.

③

④

⑧

⑨

Open at ⇨ and flatten.

◆--- Valley fold   —·— Mountain fold

⑭ Fold the topmost flap to the right.

⑮ Fold the other flaps in the same way as steps ⑫-⑭.

⑯ Unfold after marking a crease.

⑰

⑬

⑯

Make a crease.

Fold along the creases.

⑱

⑫ Fold the topmost flap to the left.

⑰ Fold over and insert the tip into the pocket ●.

Fold the other side in the same way as steps ⑧-⑩.

Fold the other side in the same way.

⑪

⑱

⑲ Open and insert the tip.

Make a crease.

Insert the tip.

B

⑩

⑲ Open and give final shape.

⑳

A

Make a crease.

Open at ◁ and flatten.

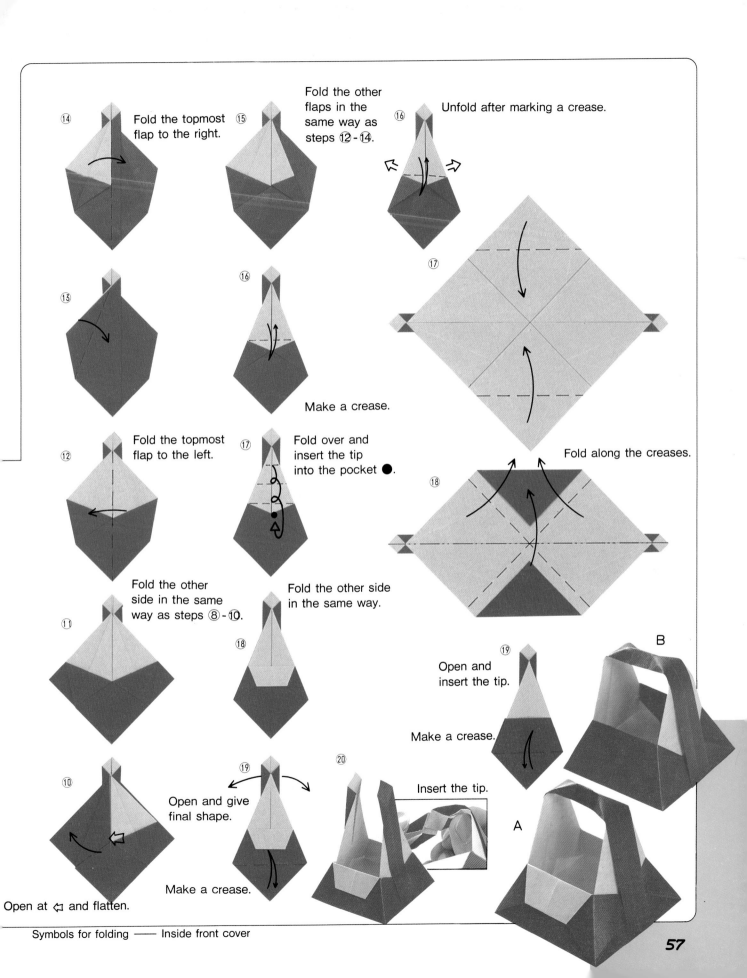

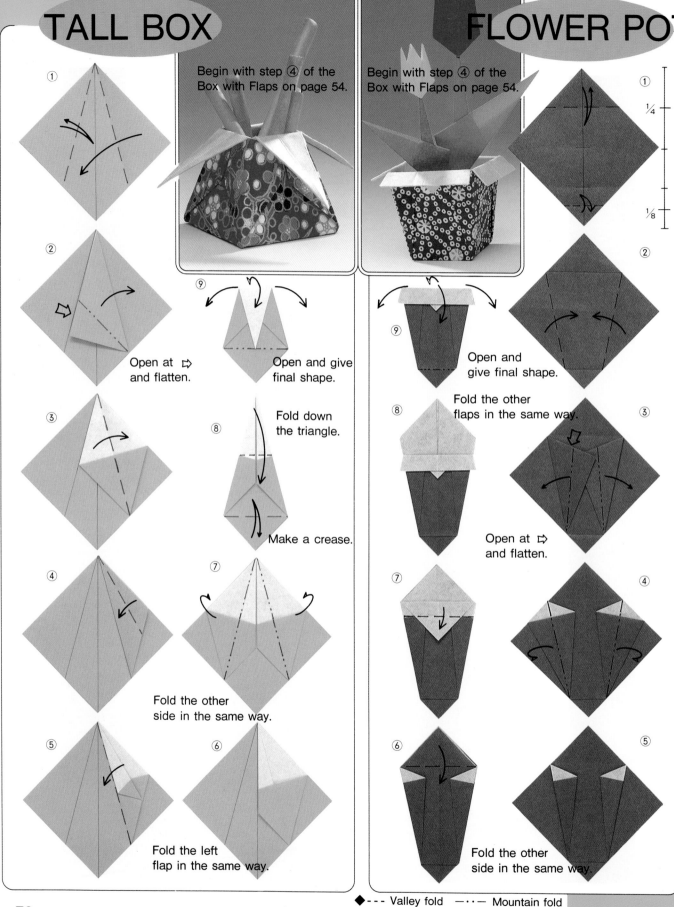

TALL BOX

FLOWER POT

① Begin with step ④ of the Box with Flaps on page 54.

Begin with step ④ of the Box with Flaps on page 54.

① ¼ ⅛

②

Open at ➡ and flatten.

⑨ Open and give final shape.

⑨ Open and give final shape.

②

③

Fold down the triangle.

⑧ Make a crease.

Fold the other flaps in the same way.

⑧

③ Open at ➡ and flatten.

④ Fold the other side in the same way.

⑦ Fold the other side in the same way.

⑦

④

⑤ Fold the left flap in the same way.

⑥

⑥

⑤ Fold the other side in the same way.

◆--- Valley fold   —·— Mountain fold

58

FOLDING PAPER-CASE

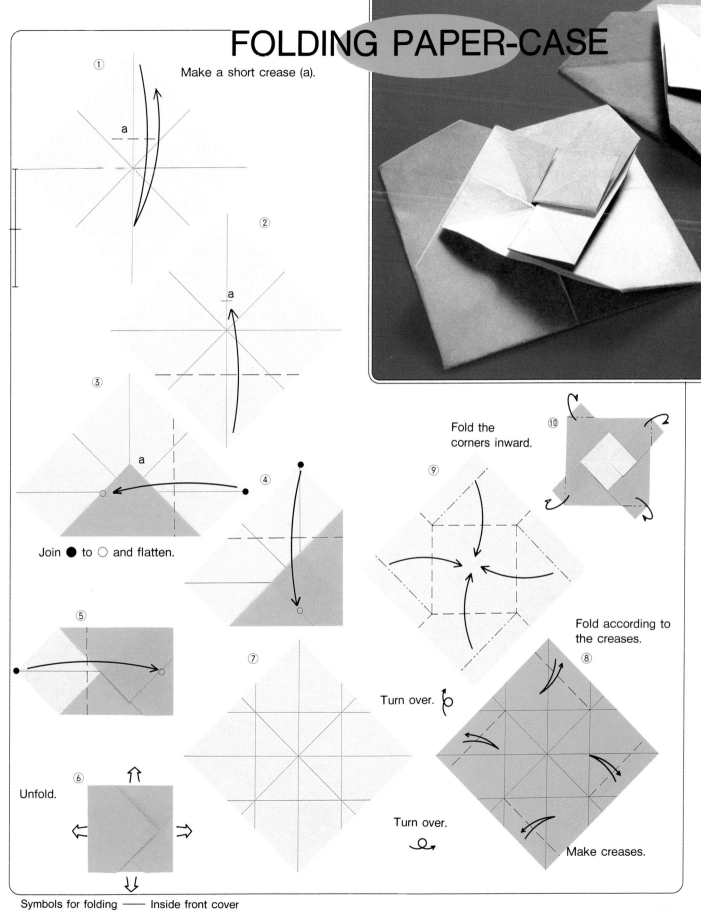

① Make a short crease (a).

a

② a

③ a

Join ● to ○ and flatten.

④

⑤

⑥ Unfold.

⑦ Turn over.

⑧ Fold according to the creases.

Make creases.

⑨ Fold the corners inward.

⑩

Symbols for folding ——— Inside front cover

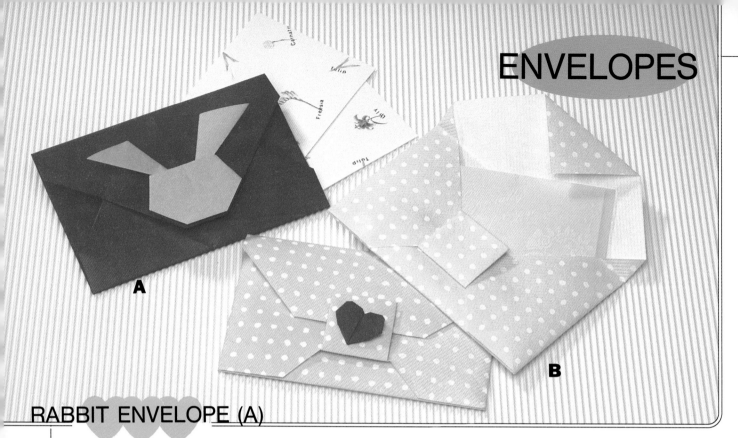

RABBIT ENVELOPE (A)

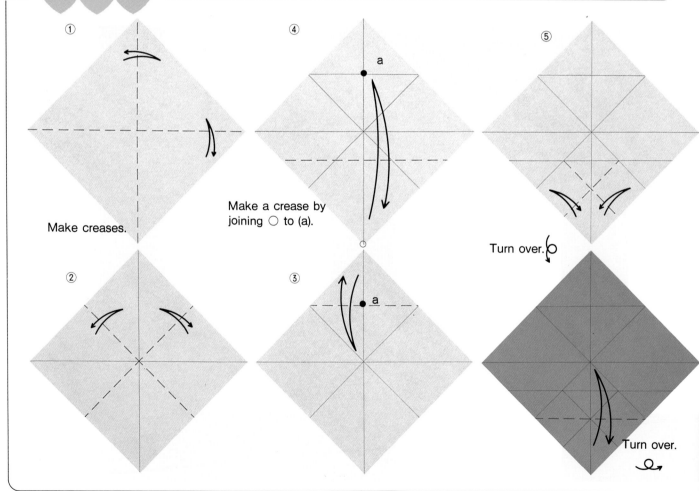

① Make creases.

②

③

④ Make a crease by joining ○ to (a).

a

⑤ Turn over.

Turn over.

◆--- Valley fold   —·— Mountain fold

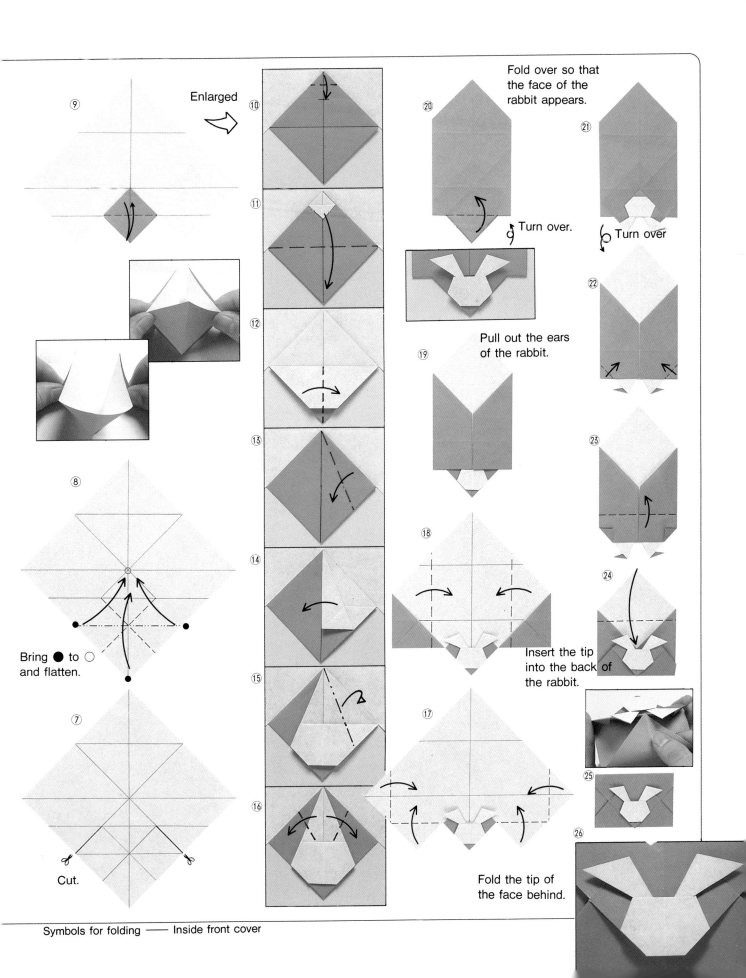

⑨

Enlarged

⑩

⑳ Fold over so that the face of the rabbit appears.

㉑

Turn over.

Turn over

⑧ Bring ● to ○ and flatten.

⑪

⑫

⑬

⑭

⑮

⑯

⑲ Pull out the ears of the rabbit.

⑱

⑰

㉒

㉓

㉔ Insert the tip into the back of the rabbit.

㉕

㉖

⑦ Cut.

Fold the tip of the face behind.

ENVELOPE(B)

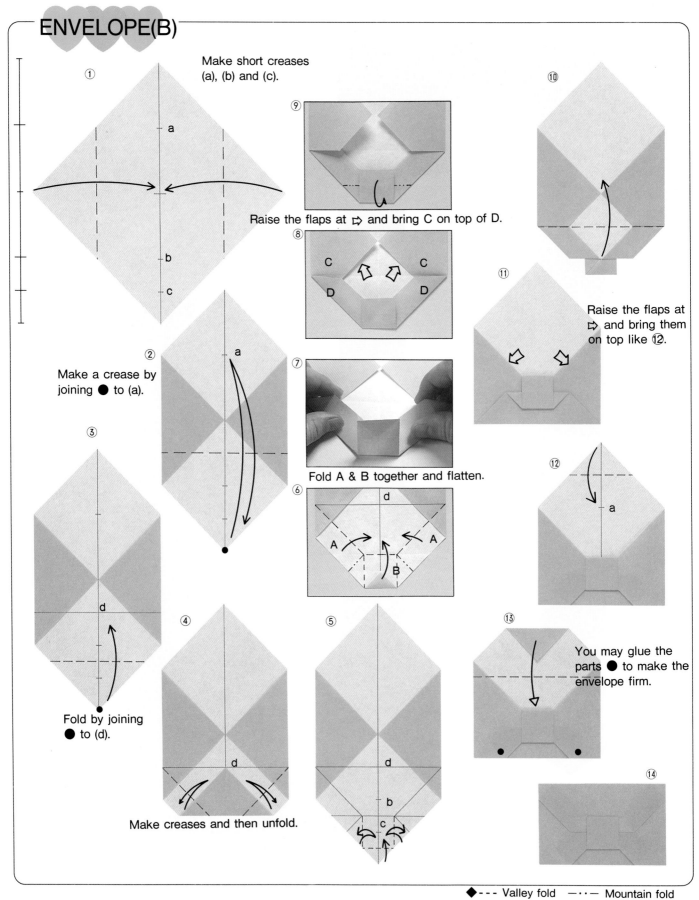

① Make short creases (a), (b) and (c).

② Make a crease by joining ● to (a).

③ Fold by joining ● to (d).

④ Make creases and then unfold.

⑤

⑥ Fold A & B together and flatten.

⑦

⑧

⑨ Raise the flaps at ➪ and bring C on top of D.

⑩

⑪ Raise the flaps at ➪ and bring them on top like ⑫.

⑫

⑬ You may glue the parts ● to make the envelope firm.

⑭

◆--- Valley fold   —·— Mountain fold

5
ORIGAMI FOR HOLIDAYS

OGRES

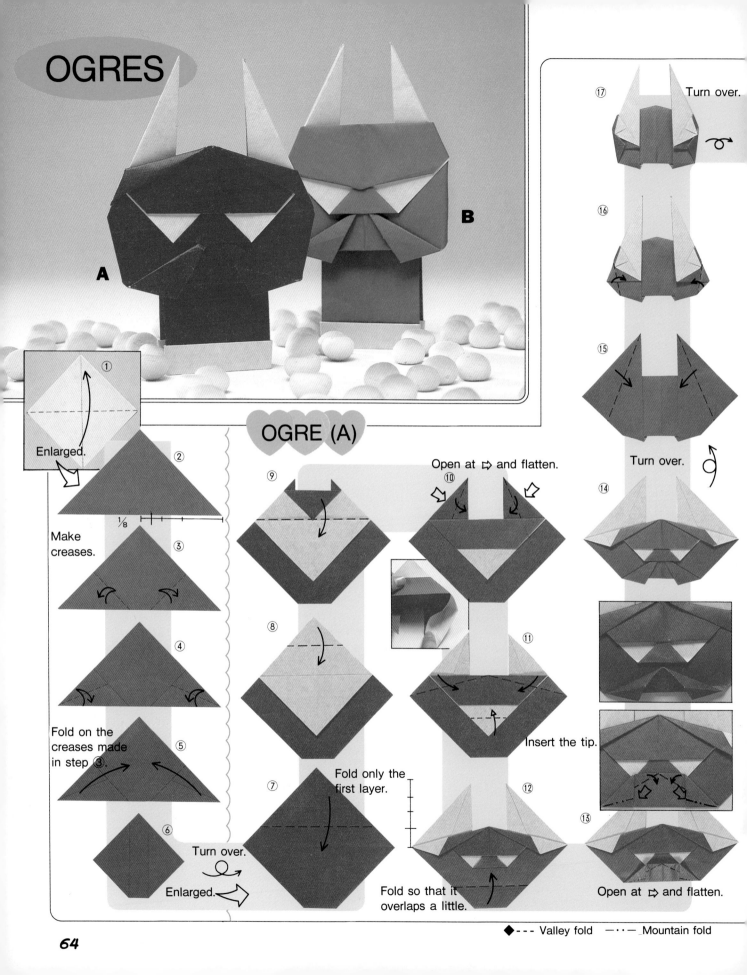

A

B

OGRE (A)

① Enlarged.

② Make creases.

⅛

③

④

⑤ Fold on the creases made in step ③.

⑥

Turn over.

Enlarged.

⑦ Fold only the first layer.

⑧

⑨

⑩ Open at ⇨ and flatten.

⑪ Insert the tip.

⑫ Fold so that it overlaps a little.

⑬ Open at ⇨ and flatten.

⑭ Turn over.

⑮ Turn over.

⑯

⑰ Turn over.

◆--- Valley fold　—·— Mountain fold

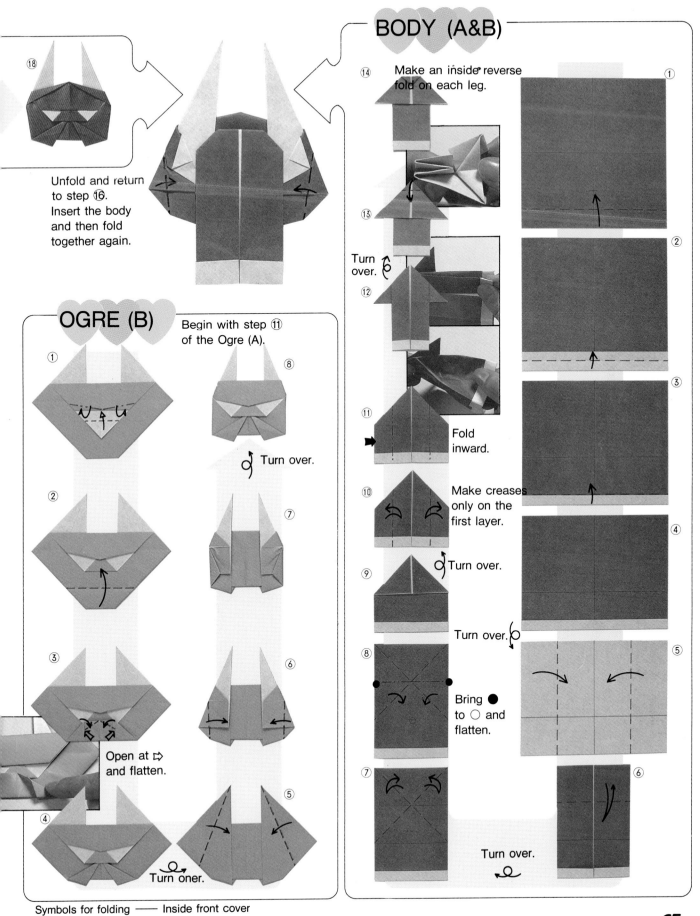

㉘

Unfold and return
to step ⑯.
Insert the body
and then fold
together again.

BODY (A&B)

⑭ Make an inside reverse
fold on each leg.

⑬

Turn
over.

⑫

⑪ Fold
inward.

⑩ Make creases
only on the
first layer.

⑨ Turn over.

⑧ Bring ●
to ○ and
flatten.

⑦

Turn over.

①
②
③
④
⑤
⑥

OGRE (B)

Begin with step ⑪
of the Ogre (A).

①

⑧

Turn over.

②
⑦

③
Open at ▷
and flatten.

⑥

④
⑤

Turn oner.

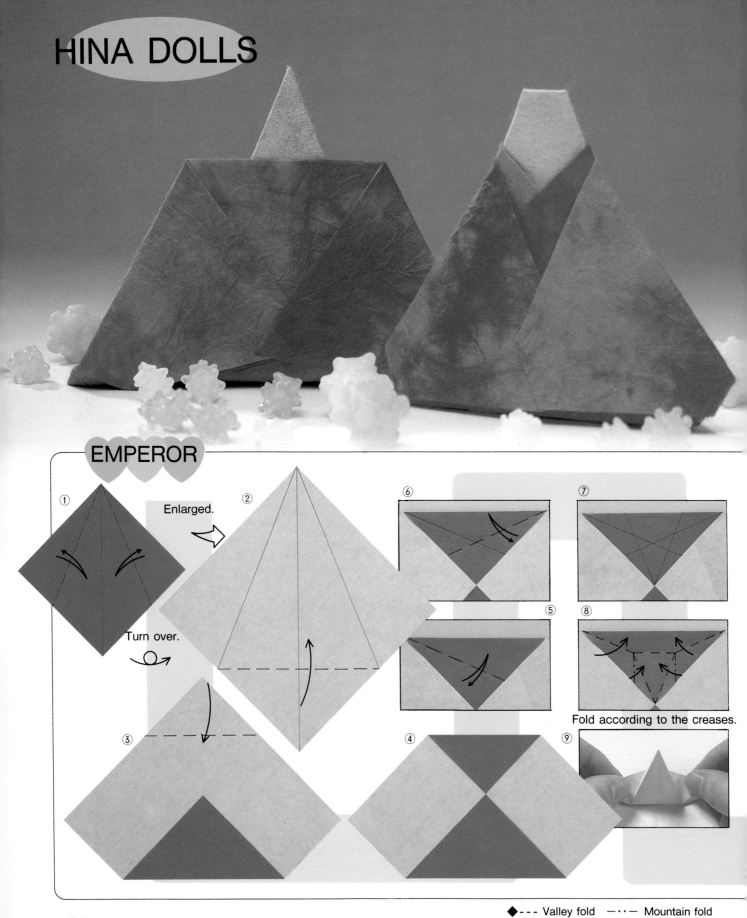

HINA DOLLS

EMPEROR

① Enlarged.

② Turn over.

③

④

⑤

⑥

⑦

⑧ Fold according to the creases.

⑨

◆--- Valley fold   —·— Mountain fold

66

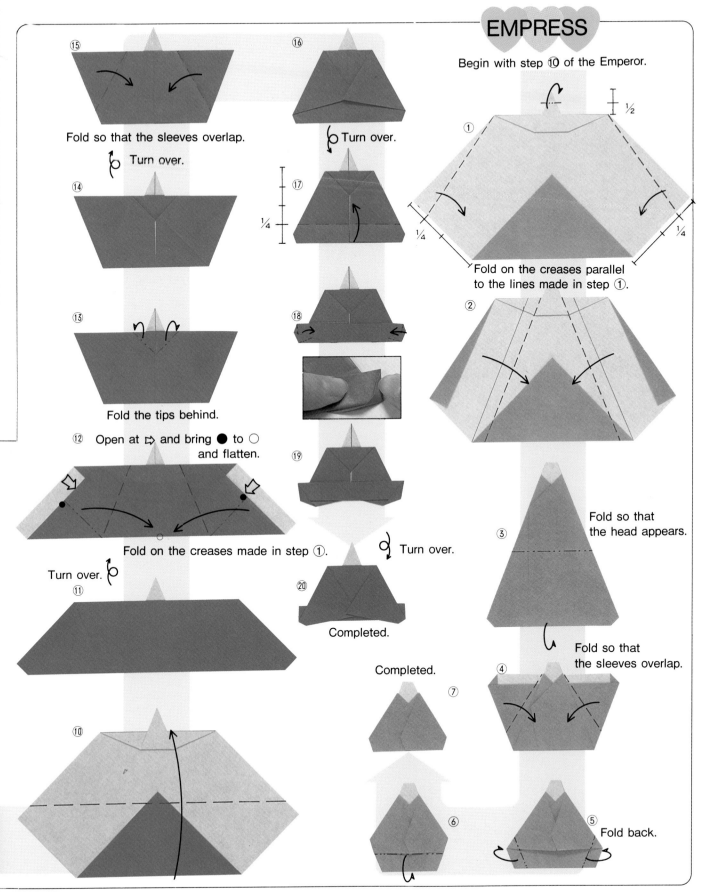

Begin with step ⑩ of the Emperor.

①
½
¼   ¼
Fold on the creases parallel
to the lines made in step ①.

②

③
Fold so that
the head appears.

④
Fold so that
the sleeves overlap.

⑤
Fold back.

⑥

⑦
Completed.

⑮
Fold so that the sleeves overlap.
Turn over.

⑭

⑬
Fold the tips behind.

⑫ Open at ⇨ and bring ● to ○
and flatten.
Fold on the creases made in step ①.

Turn over.
⑪

⑩

⑯
Turn over.

⑰
¼

⑱

⑲
Turn over.

⑳
Completed.

EMPEROR

① Make creases.

② Mark (a) and then (b).

Turn over.

b

a

③ Fold to (b).

b

EMPRESS

Begin with step ⑪ of the Emperor.

①

②

③

④

⑤ Make creases as in steps ⑭-⑰ of the Emperor. Fold A, B and C and flatten.

C   C

B   B

A

⑥ Insert the tip of the skirt under the coat.

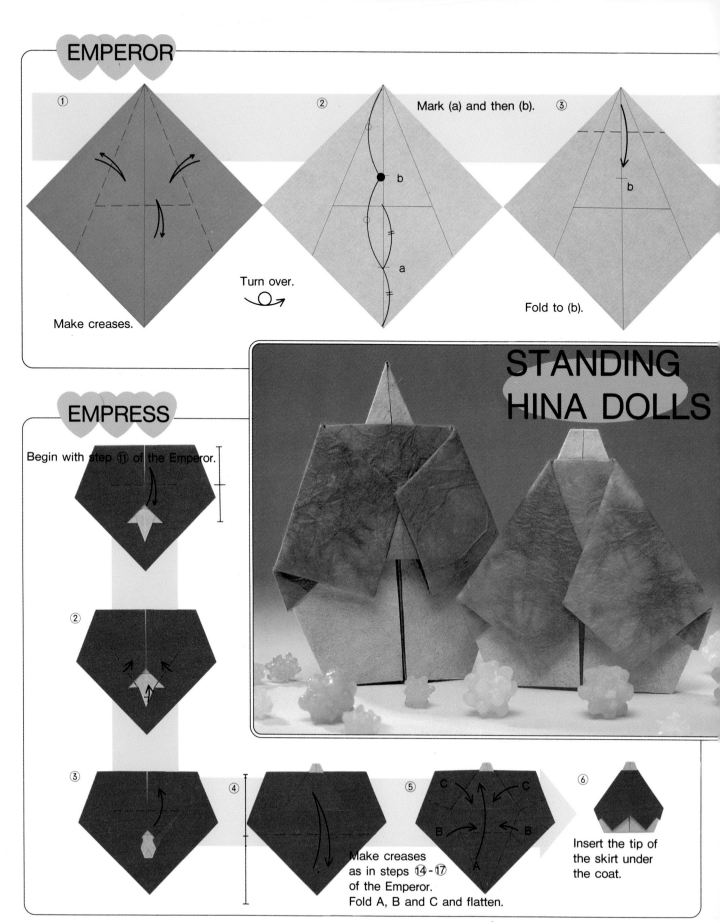

STANDING HINA DOLLS

◆--- Valley fold   —·—·— Mountain fold

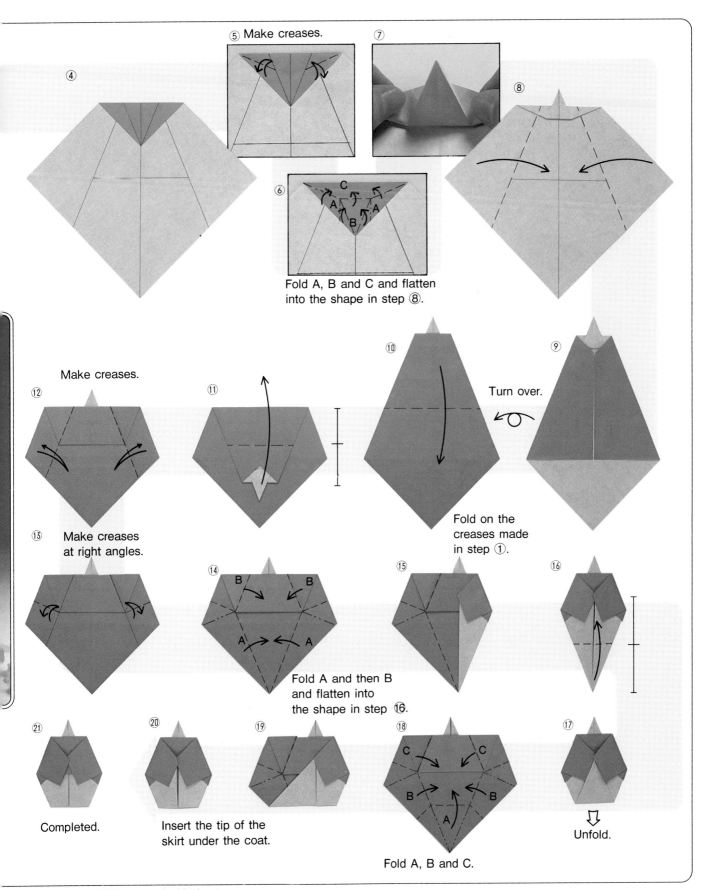

⑤ Make creases.

⑦

④

⑥ Fold A, B and C and flatten
into the shape in step ⑧.

⑧

Make creases.

⑫

⑪

⑩ Fold on the
creases made
in step ①.

Turn over.

⑨

Make creases
at right angles.

⑬

⑭ Fold A and then B
and flatten into
the shape in step ⑯.

⑮

⑯

㉑ Completed.

⑳ Insert the tip of the
skirt under the coat.

⑲

⑱ Fold A, B and C.

⑰ Unfold.

CARP STREAMER

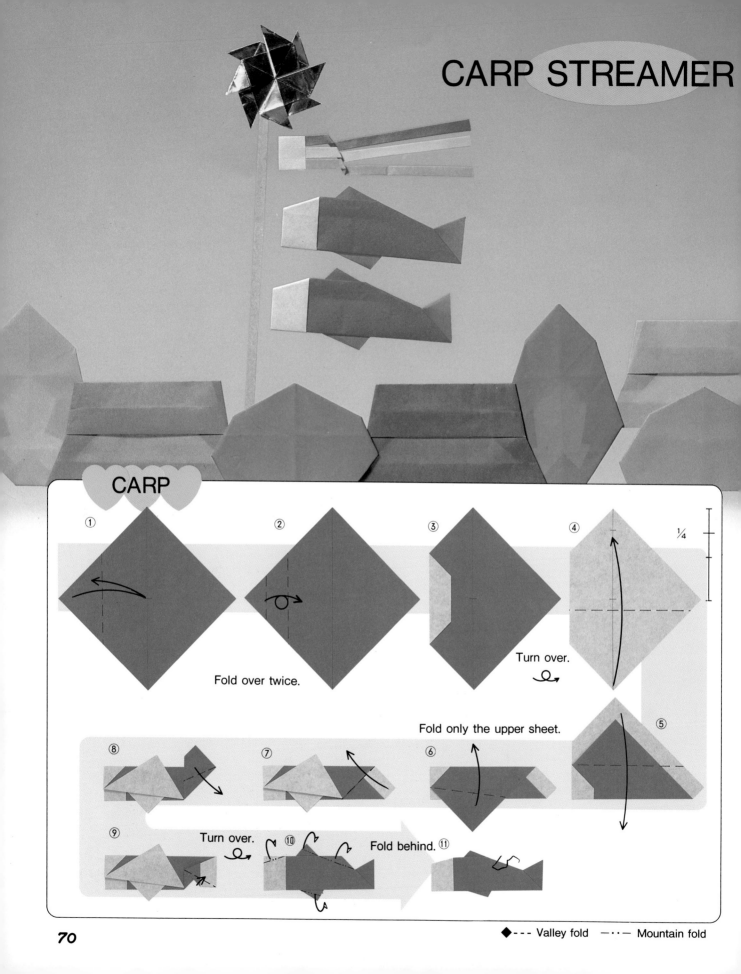

CARP

① Fold over twice.

②

③

④ ¼

Turn over.

⑤ Fold only the upper sheet.

⑥

⑦

⑧

⑨ Turn over.

⑩ Fold behind.

⑪

◆--- Valley fold   —·— Mountain fold

STREAMER

Fold three strips of paper as shown.

① ② ③

Glue the ends together.

WHEEL

Make two Windmills on page 45 and glue together.

① ② ③

POLE

Fold a long and narrow piece of paper.

① ②

ROOF

① ② ③ ④

Move a little in the direction of the arrows and fold.

⑥ ⑤ Turn over.

⑧ ⑦ Turn over.

TREE (A)

① ② ③ ④ ⑤ ⑥ Turn over.

TREE (B)

① ② ③ ④ ⑤ ⑥ Turn over.

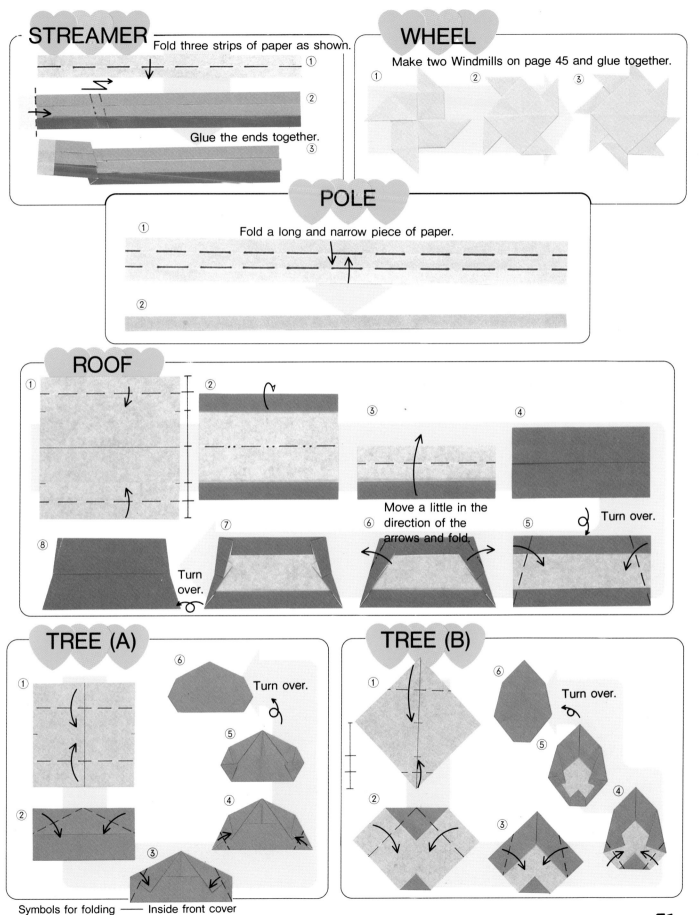

Symbols for folding —— Inside front cover

HELMETS

A

B

HELMET (Traditional)

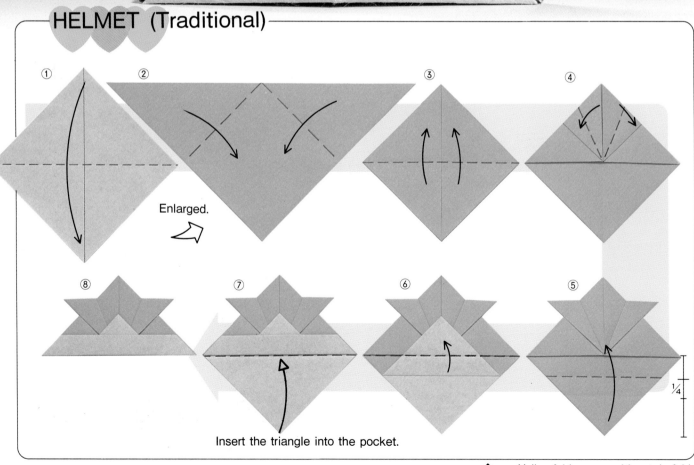

① ② Enlarged. ③ ④

⑤ ⑥ ⑦ ⑧

¼

Insert the triangle into the pocket.

◆--- Valley fold   —·— Mountain fold

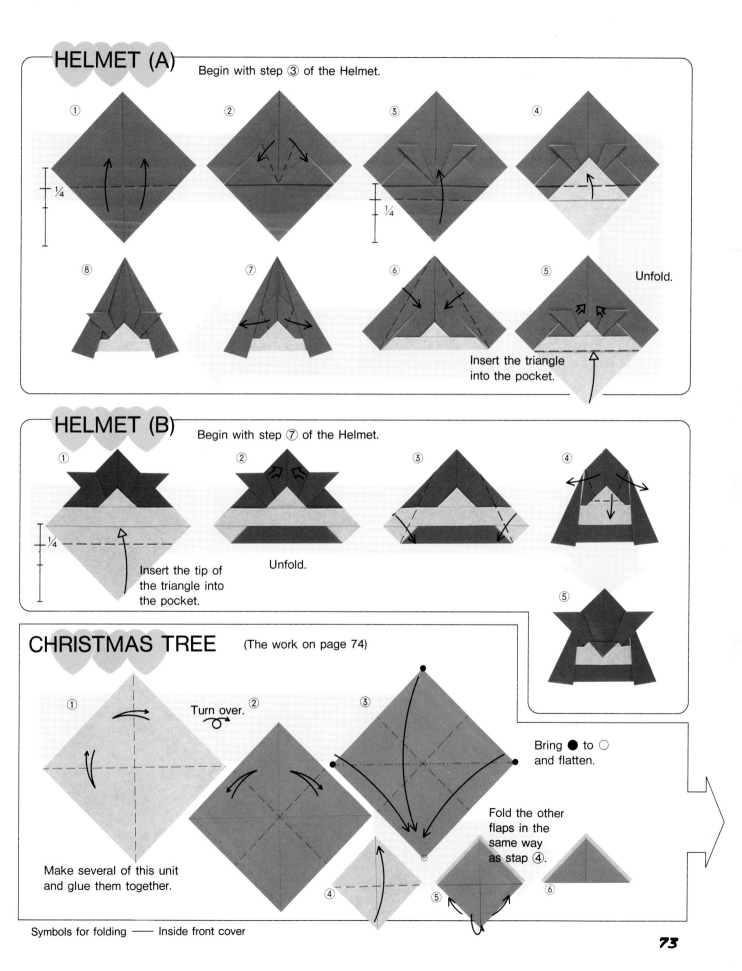

HELMET (A)

Begin with step ③ of the Helmet.

①

②

③

④

¼

¼

⑧

⑦

⑥

⑤

Unfold.

Insert the triangle into the pocket.

HELMET (B)

Begin with step ⑦ of the Helmet.

①

¼

Insert the tip of the triangle into the pocket.

②

Unfold.

③

④

⑤

CHRISTMAS TREE

(The work on page 74)

①

Turn over.

②

③

Bring ● to ○ and flatten.

Make several of this unit and glue them together.

④

Fold the other flaps in the same way as stap ④.

⑤

⑥

Symbols for folding —— Inside front cover

SANTA CLAUS

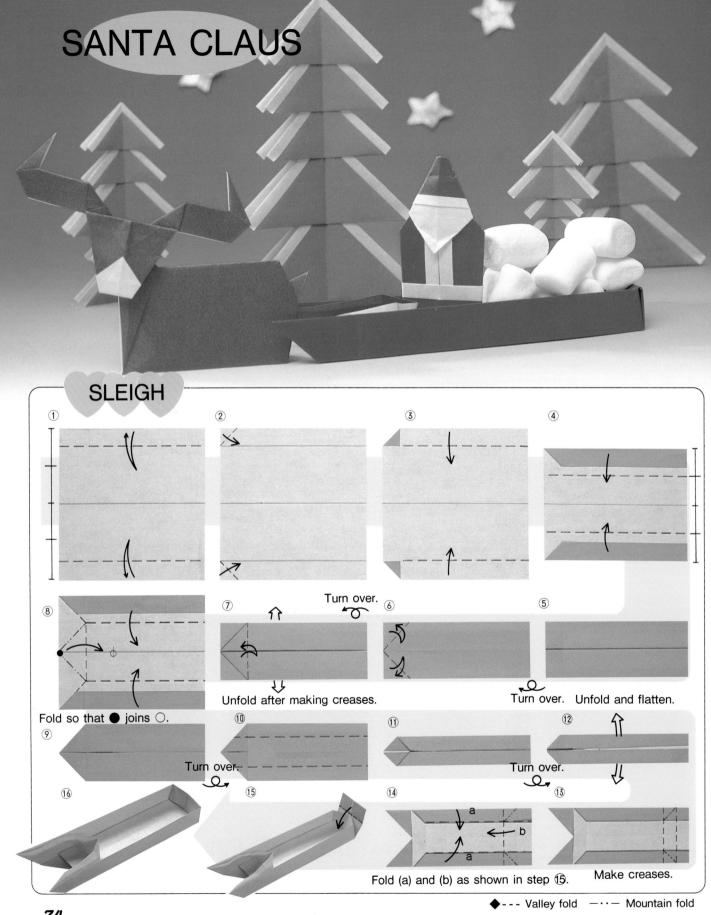

SLEIGH

① ② ③ ④

⑧

Fold so that ● joins ○.

Turn over.

⑦ ⑥ ⑤

Unfold after making creases.

Turn over. Unfold and flatten.

⑨ ⑩ ⑪ ⑫

Turn over.

Turn over.

⑯ ⑮ ⑭ ⑬

a

← b

a

Fold (a) and (b) as shown in step ⑮.

Make creases.

◆--- Valley fold —·—· Mountain fold

See page 73 for the Christmas Tree.
See pages 78-79 for Star.
See page 9 for the Reindeer.

The paper before folding

The proportional length
of the head to body
is 1 to 1.5.

HEAD   BODY

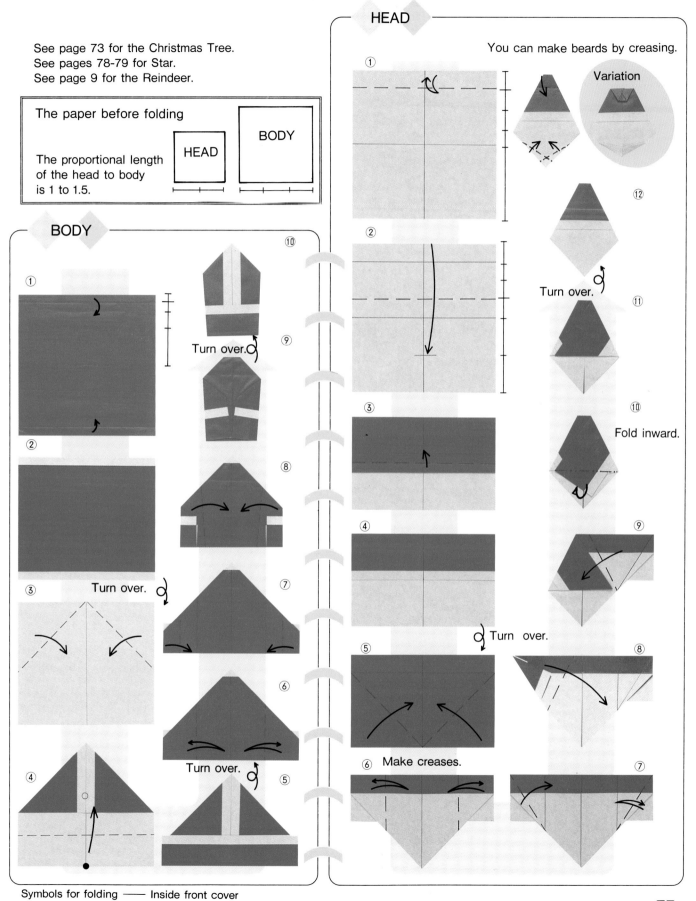

BODY

① ② ③ Turn over. ④ ⑤ Turn over. ⑥ ⑦ ⑧ ⑨ Turn over. ⑩

HEAD

You can make beards by creasing.

Variation

① ② ③ ④ ⑤ Turn over. ⑥ Make creases. ⑦ ⑧ ⑨ ⑩ Fold inward. ⑪ Turn over. ⑫

BODY

BOY

GIRL

①

Turn over.

②

Turn over.

②

③

Turn over.

③

④

④

⑤

Turn over.

Turn over.

⑤

⑥

⑥

⑦

⑦

A

①

②

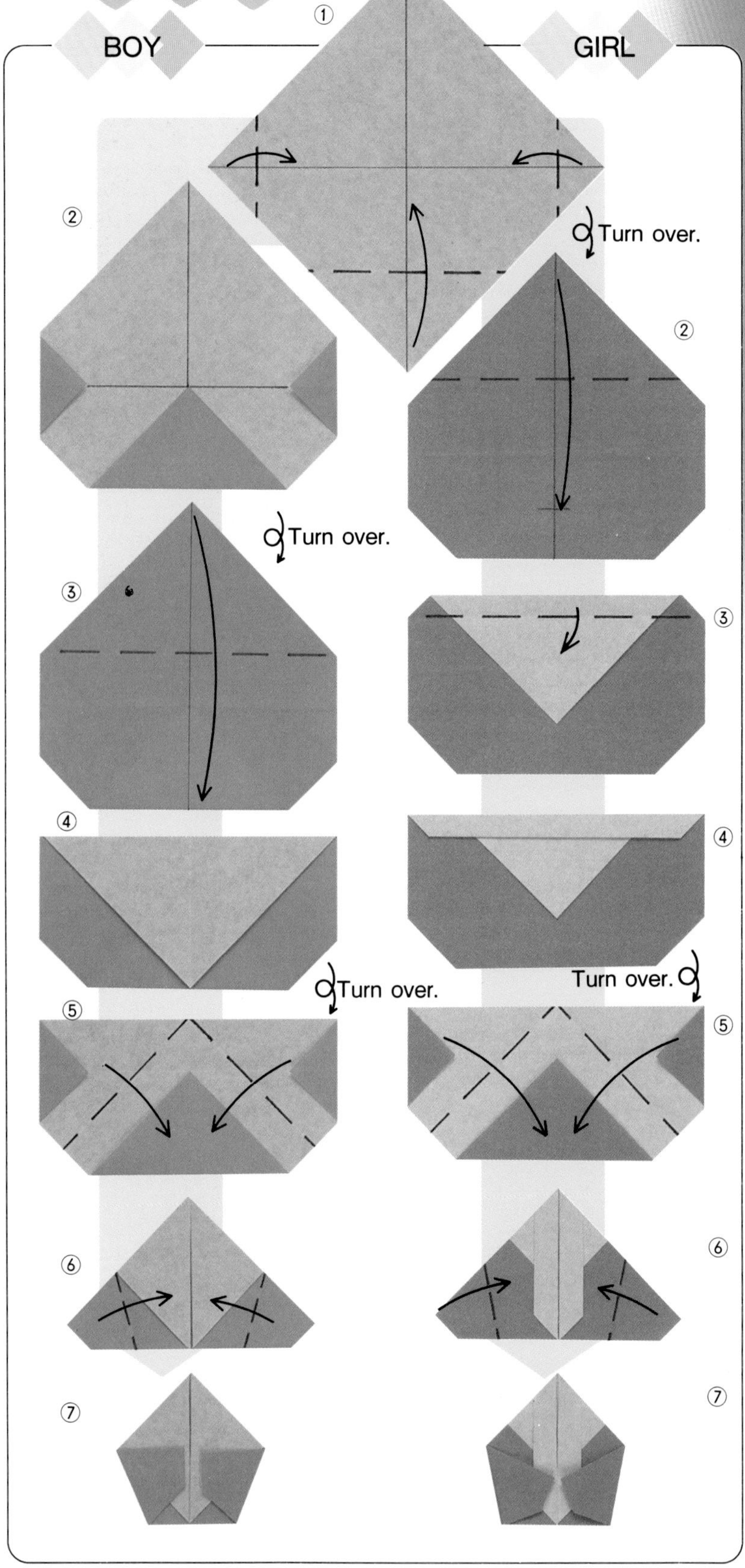

HEAD

Begin with step ⑫ of the Santa Clause on page 75.

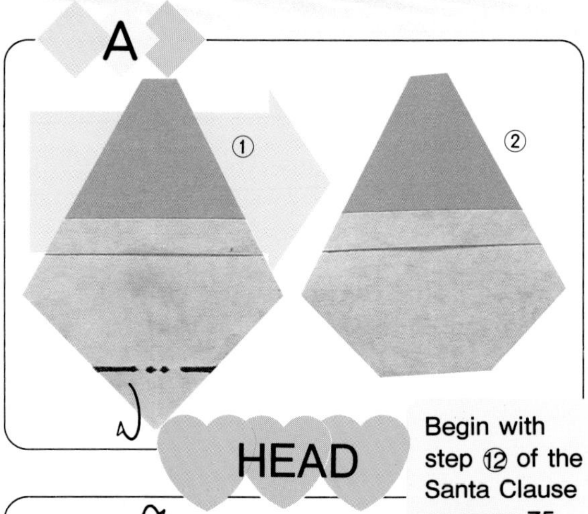

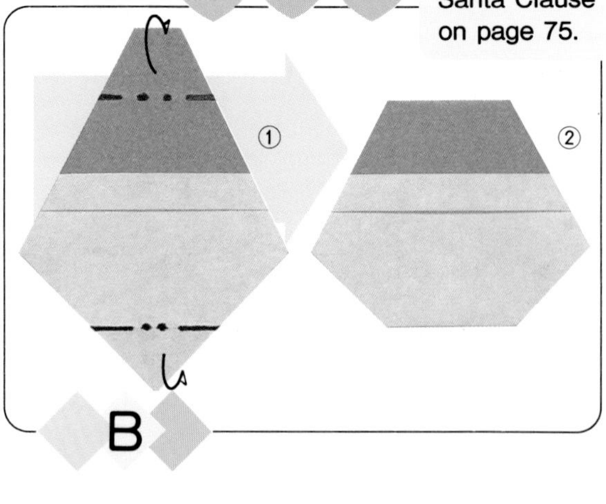

①

②

B

76

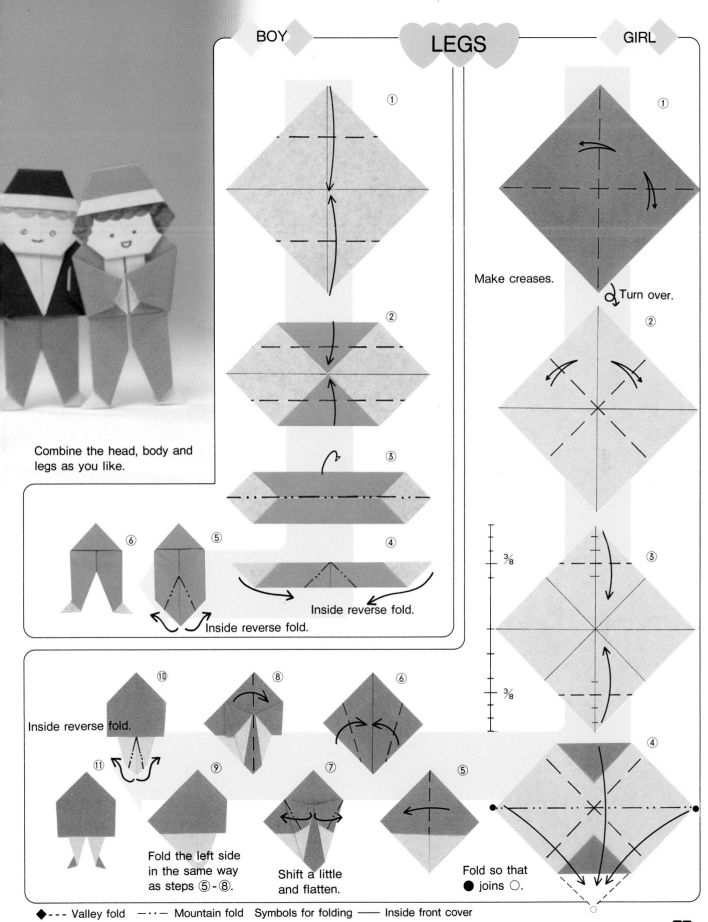

①

②

③

④

Inside reverse fold.

⑤

⑥

Inside reverse fold.

Combine the head, body and legs as you like.

Make creases.

Turn over.

①

②

③

⅜

⅜

④

⑤

Fold so that ● joins ○.

Inside reverse fold.

⑩

⑪

⑨

⑧

⑦

⑥

Fold the left side in the same way as steps ⑤ - ⑧.

Shift a little and flatten.

◆--- Valley fold   —·— Mountain fold   Symbols for folding   —— Inside front cover

77

HEART

See page 60 for the completed work.

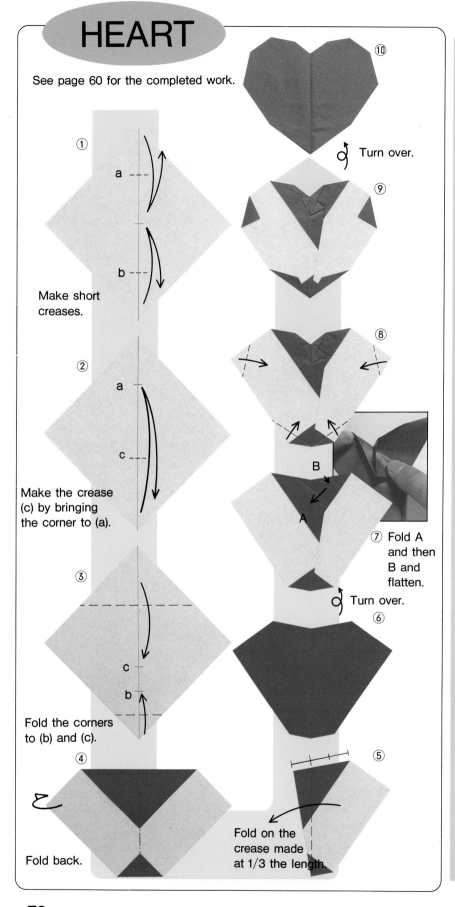

① a ----

b ----

Make short creases.

② a ----

c ----

Make the crease (c) by bringing the corner to (a).

③ c ----

b ----

Fold the corners to (b) and (c).

④

Fold back.

⑩ Turn over.

⑨

⑧

B

A

⑦ Fold A and then B and flatten.

Turn over.

⑥

⑤ Fold on the crease made at 1/3 the length.

HOW TO MAKE A PENTAGON

①

②

③

④ a ● Mark (a).

⑤ a ● Bring line (b) to (a).

b ●

⑥

Fold behind.

◆--- Valley fold   —·— Mountain fold

78

STAR

Completed works are on pages 74 & 80.

Begin with the Pentagon.

① Make creases.

Bring (b) to (a) and then (c) and (d).

②

③ Fold 4 flaps to the left.

④ Make creases at 1/4 the length.

⑤ Fold 3 flaps to the right.

⑥ Open at ⇨ and fold along the creases made in step ④.

⑦

⑧ Turn over.

Fold A and then B.

⑨ Fold the other corners in the same way.

⑩

Turn over.

⑪ Completed.

⑫

⑪ Unfold.

⑩ Cut.

⑨

⑧

⑦

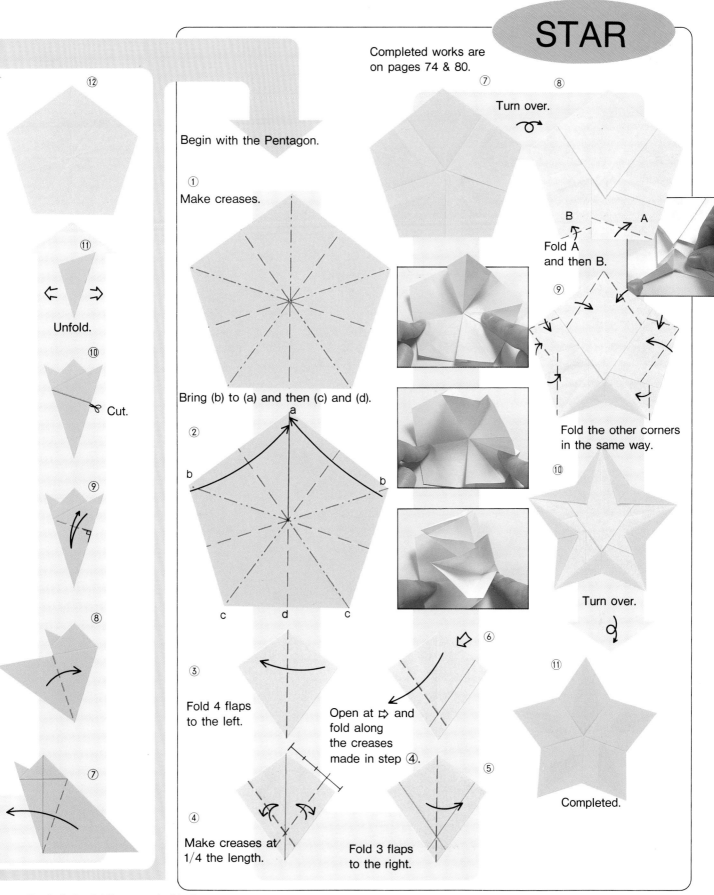

DECORATIONS

FOR CHRISTMAS

FOR BIRTHDAY

FOR THE STAR FESTIVAL

See page 79 for the Star.

LEAF

① ② ③ ④

WREATH

① Fold 8 leaves to make the wreath.

Unfold.

② Make creases.

③ Glue the leaf along the crease.

④

Fold the upper layer.

Glue the flowers as you like.

FLOWER

① Bring ● to ○ and flatten. (See page 42.)

② ③ ④

◆--- Valley fold   —·—· Mountain fold   Symbols for folding   —— Inside front cover